INCREDIBLE

SUPER BOWL ACTION

by
Angelo Resciniti
and
Ann Steinberg

To my super grandfolks, Angelo and Rose Resciniti. They took me to the first Super Bowl game. And they gave me love, always. May God bless them both.
And to M.H. for a super opportunity.
Thanks.
A.R. to R.E., for removing the albatross.
Thanks.

A.S.

Published by Willowisp Press, Inc.
10100 SBF Drive, Pinellas Park, FL 34666

Copyright ©1991 by Willowisp Press, Inc.

Printed in the United States of America

2 4 6 8 10 9 7 5 3 1

ISBN 0-87406-276-4

CONTENTS

SUPER BOWL QUIZ

1. Which teams have won more Super Bowls than any other teams? How many?

2. Which teams have played in more Super Bowls than any other teams? How many?

3. Which teams have won two Super Bowls in a row?

4. In which Super Bowl were the most points scored? The fewest?

5. Who are the only two players to be named Most Valuable Player two years in a row? Which player has won the MVP award three times?

6. Who is the only player from a losing team to win MVP honors?

7. When did two players win the MVP award? Who were they?

8. Who has thrown the most touchdown passes in a Super Bowl game?

9. Which stadium has hosted the Super Bowl more times than any other?

10. Many defenses have had colorful nicknames. Which Super Bowl team featured the *Purple People-Eaters? The Steel Curtain? The Orange Crush? The Doomsday Defense? The Killer Bees?*

(The answers are on page 191.)

SUPER BOWL XXV

BUFFALO vs. NEW YORK GIANTS

Could the defense of the New York Giants, number one in the NFL, stop the high-flying offense of Jim Kelly and his Buffalo Bills? That was the question every football fan was asking before Super Bowl XXV.

The underdog Giants were pinning their hopes on their punishing "D." Everyone knew their offense was no match for the Bills' overpowering attack. During the regular season, Buffalo's 428 points topped the NFL. The Giants, on the other hand, often had trouble punching the ball into the end zone.

New York's season got off to a great start. When the team won its first 10 games, Giant fans were dreaming of recapturing the glory of their 1986 championship year. But a loss to Philadelphia sent the Giants into a tailspin. They could manage only a field goal, losing 7-3, in a bitterly fought defensive struggle against the 49ers. Then disaster struck.

Starting QB Phil Simms went down with a season-ending injury in a late-season loss to Buffalo. The Giants' hopes now rode with substitute QB Jeff Hostetler, who had started only two games in his whole NFL career. Not many people expected much from the second-stringer.

Jim Kelly, the Bills' signal-caller, was having his best season. He was the top-rated passer in the league. Even more important than his powerful arm was his ability to make the right decision under pressure. Kelly was the only NFL quarterback who called all his own plays. He led Buffalo's "hurry-up" attack, the most feared weapon in the NFL. Operating without a huddle, Kelly would survey the defense, decide which play to call to attack it best, and then speed into action before the defense could make any changes. The usual result was confusion for the defenders—and lots of points for the Bills!

The Bills rumbled through the play-offs like a stampeding buffalo. They annihilated the Miami Dolphins and the Los Angeles Raiders by a combined score of 95-37. In the AFC title game against L.A., Kelly threw for 300 yards in a 51-3 laugher. The Bills' brilliant running back Thurman Thomas darted for 138 rushing yards. Veteran wide receiver James Lofton caught five passes for 113 yards and two TDs. And fullback Kenneth Davis bulled his way into the end zone three times. The Bills looked invincible.

The Giants won their first play-off game with surprising ease, battering the Chicago Bears 31-3. But that meant they would have to face a much tougher test—the NFC championship game against the two-time defending Super Bowl champ San Francisco 49ers. The 'Niners were going for a "three-peat"—to win three Super Bowls in a row. No other team had ever done it.

But the Giant defense, pressuring and blitzing all day long, held superstar QB Joe Montana to only 190 yards in the air. Then Montana left the game with a broken hand, with San Francisco leading 13-12 late in the fourth quarter. After a critical 49er fumble, Hostetler coolly moved his Giants into field goal range. With four seconds remaining, placekicker Matt Bahr, who already had four field goals, came on the field for one more try. Many of his teammates kneeled in prayer, afraid to look. But the kick sailed through the uprights and the Giants were winners. Unknown Jeff Hostetler, with only 158 throws in the pros, had led them to victory against perhaps the greatest team and greatest quarterback of all time.

"They keep telling me I can't do it. Now

I'm going to the Super Bowl!" Hostetler said with a grin after the game.

There was a dark cloud hanging over this silver anniversary Super Bowl. The U.S. was at war in the Persian Gulf. While the country anxiously awaited news from the battlefront, extraordinary measures were taken to protect the Super Bowl from a terrorist attack.

As the 73,813 fans filed into Tampa Stadium, every one of them had to pass through a metal detector. Extra fences, concrete barriers, SWAT teams, horses, dogs and 2,000 security guards were in place to prevent a tragedy. Everything went without a hitch. No one was hurt. Nothing could dampen the enthusiasm of the fans.

The crowd was expecting early fireworks when the Bills won the coin toss. Buffalo had a perfect 7-0 record when they scored first. And they had scored TDs on their first possession in nine of their last 12 games. "Our first defensive series, we've got to go out and stop them in three plays," said Giant nose tackle Erik Howard before the game.

Stop them in three plays is just what the Giants did. Then New York went to work on offense, driving 58 yards in 11 plays, while holding on to the ball for 6:15. Matt Bahr's 28-yard field goal gave the Giants an early 3-0 lead. But it took the Bills only 83 seconds to tie it up. A 61-yard pass to Lofton led to Scott Norwood's 23-yard field goal. At the beginning of the second quarter, the Bills grabbed the lead. An 80-yard drive ended with a Don Smith plunge into the end zone. 10-3, Buffalo.

Jeff Hostetler was off to a shaky start. His throws were off. The Bill defenders were pounding him. And on the Giants' next possession, Buffalo defensive end Leon Seals, whose hard but clean hit had put Simms out of action during the season, almost ended Hostetler's season, too. On a fierce pass rush, Seals flattened the Giant QB. Hostetler was so shaken up he needed smelling salts. Third-string quarterback Matt Cavenaugh started to warm up.

But Hostetler stayed in the game. The next time he had the ball, he faded back to pass from his own 7-yard line. He tripped over teammate Ottis Anderson's foot and stumbled. Buffalo All-Pro end Bruce Smith grabbed Hostetler's arm and threw him down in the end zone for a safety. Fans were amazed that Hostetler, dazed from Seals' hit on the previous series, was able to hold onto the ball and not fumble. But things looked bad enough for New York, now down 12-3.

Bruce Smith, who played against Hostetler in college, wasn't at all surprised at the

MVP Ottis Anderson rambles for some of his 102 yards in Super Bowl XXV.

Photo Allsport U.S.A.

quarterback's determination. "He's tough as nails," said Smith later. "Once I knocked him out, and he got up and took one step and fell down again. Then he got up, and three plays later threw a touchdown pass!"

With the safety, momentum was with the Bills. But the usually reliable Andre Reed, Buffalo's outstanding wide receiver, suddenly became Mr. Butterfingers. He dropped several wide-open passes. When he finally held on to one, Giants' linebacker Carl Banks blasted him just as he caught the ball and stopped him just short of a critical first down.

Fired up by the tough defense, Hostetler began to move. After a terrific 18-yard run by Anderson, the Giant QB hit Mark Ingram for 22 yards. Dave Meggett ran for 17 more. Then tight end Howard Cross made a great catch on his knees to keep the drive alive. Two plays later, wideout Stephen Baker caught Hostetler's floater in the corner of the end zone. With just 25 seconds left in the half, the Giants had closed to within two, 12-10.

The Giants knew they were lucky to be trailing by only two at halftime. They opened the second half with the most time-consuming scoring drive in Super Bowl history. The 75-yard drive took 9:29 off the clock. But when the drive ended with Ottis Anderson's TD plunge, the Giants led 17-12. Then, late in the third quarter, with the Bills on the Giant 31, the spectacular Thurman Thomas slipped through a hole in the Giant line, fought off several tackles, and raced in for a score. The Bills had clawed back to a 19-17 lead.

The explosiveness of the Bills' drive recalled a remark Thomas had made earlier in the week. He described the only disadvantage of the no-huddle offense. "We get the ball, drive for the touchdown, go back to the bench, and look up at the scoreboard, and you haven't taken any time off the clock."

The Giants had a different style. They were eating up the clock for lunch! During one 17-1/2-minute stretch, they held the ball for all but two minutes. Exhausted from spending so much time on the field, the Buffalo defenders were starting to miss tackles. "It definitely did take a toll on us," explained Bills linebacker Cornelius Bennett after the game. "When you get tired, you start making a lot of arm tackles."

The Giants were set to grind it out once more. His confidence growing with each play, Hostetler led his team 74 yards downfield in 14 plays. But the Buffalo defense somehow was able to stop New York after first and goal at the 3. After holding the ball for another 7:32, the Giants had to settle for a Matt Bahr field goal. They led 20-19.

The stage was set for a Super Bowl heart-stopper! With 2:12 left in the game, Buffalo started on its own 10. With Kelly passing and scrambling and Thomas darting and dashing, the Bills moved swiftly downfield. With everyone thinking "pass," Thomas took a hand-off and blazed down to the Giant 29. But they were out of timeouts. Kelly killed the clock by slamming the ball into the ground. Eight seconds were left. Scott Norwood came in to try the biggest FG of his life.

The Giants tried to psych him out by calling time. The kick would have to travel 47 yards, matching Norwood's longest field goal of the year. It was right on the edge of his range. Giant kicker Matt Bahr knew how Norwood felt. "A 47-yard field goal is a tough kick, let alone at the end of a Super Bowl," he said.

The teams lined up. The kick sailed toward the uprights. It had the distance. But it faded two yards to the right. The New York Giants, the team no one thought could do it, were Super Bowl champs.

"You don't get a second chance," said a devastated Scott Norwood in the quiet Buffalo locker room after the game. "I let a lot of people down. I'm sure it will never get to a point where I'll ever forget it."

In the Giants' locker room, things were different. "Power wins football games!" shouted

Giant coach Bill Parcells. He was right. The Giants' defense had stopped the Bills' offense. Using only two down linemen and five or six defensive backs, the Giants had given Kelly time to throw. But they never left any of his receivers open.

But the Giant offense had come through, too, in a way not many people expected. They had more total yards, more passing yards, and more rushing yards than the Bills. They converted nine of 16 third downs, while the Bills made only one of eight. But the incredible stat was time of possession. New York's ball-control offense had held the ball for a staggering 40:33, a Super Bowl record.

Jeff Hostetler, the most inexperienced Super Bowl QB in history, completed 20 of 32 passes for 222 yards, a touchdown, and had no interceptions. Ottis Anderson, the Giants' 34-year-old running back carried the ball 21 times for 102 yards and a TD. He had been the guy the Giants went to throughout the season when they needed the tough yards. He was named MVP of the silver anniversary Super Bowl XXV.

Anderson had a marvelous game, no doubt about it. But if Scott Norwood's last kick had been good and the Bills had gone home winners, the MVP would have been Thurman Thomas. The Bills' running back averaged 9.5

yards *every time* he touched the ball! He carried the ball 15 times for 135 yards and caught five passes for 55 more yards.

The Super Bowl XXV had been the closest in history. Many people thought it was the best of all, too. "It came down to the last kick," said Jim Kelly, "and the Super Bowl is supposed to be played that way."

No fan could disagree.

Buffalo	3	9	0	7	—	19
New York	3	7	7	3	—	20

NY   —FG Bahr 28
Buffalo—FG Norwood 23
Buffalo—D. Smith 1 run (Norwood kick)
Buffalo—Safety, Hostetler tackled in end zone by B. Smith
NY   —Baker 14 pass from Hostetler (Bahr kick)
NY   —Anderson 1 run (Bahr kick)
Buffalo—Thomas 31 run (Norwood kick)
NY   —FG Bahr 21

SUPER BOWL XXIV

SAN FRANCISCO vs. DENVER

Were the San Francisco 49ers the greatest team in gridiron history?

Everybody was asking the same question before Super Bowl XXIV. The 'Niners had more wins than anybody in the 1980s. Now they were trying to win back-to-back Super Bowls—something that hadn't been done since the Pittsburgh Steelers pulled it off in Super Bowls XIII and XIV. And another triumph would give the 'Niners four Super Bowl trophies—only the proud Steelers could match that.

They would meet the Denver Broncos. The Super Bowl records of the two teams were exact opposites. San Francisco had won three and lost none. The Broncos had played in three Super Bowls—and had been blown out in all three!

Still, no one was counting out a team with a lethal weapon like quarterback John Elway.

16

Denver's flamethrower had one of the strongest arms in the game. He had no equal when throwing on the run. Like his 'Niner counterpart Joe Montana, Elway was famous for making the big play at crunch time when the game was on the line.

The two quarterbacks had very different styles. Montana was cool, precise, totally in charge all the time. There were other NFL quarterbacks with stronger arms and quicker releases. But Montana's accuracy was deadly. No QB in history was ever better at hitting second, third, and fourth receivers when the primary receiver was covered. And everyone knew Montana was a winner.

Elway was the more gifted athlete. His strength, speed, and golden arm had earmarked him for greatness early on. He was the number-one draft pick in the nation when he came out of Stanford in 1983. His playmaking had engineered heart-pounding wins for the Broncos. Few fans would ever forget his rifle—TD pass to Mark Jackson to tie the 1986 AFC championship game against the Cleveland Browns with just 39 seconds left. Or the brilliant overtime march down a muddy field to victory in that game.

But in the biggest games of his career— Super Bowls XXI and XXII against less-heralded quarterbacks Phil Simms of the

Giants and Doug Williams of the Redskins—
Elway's team had been outscored 81-30.
Would John Elway make up for those games
in his third try for the big one?

Those people who thought that Denver, 12-
point underdogs, had a chance pointed to the
improved Bronco defense. The Bronco defender had been pushed around in the past,
but now they were bigger, tougher, and
stronger. The season before, the Broncos had
been ranked 27th of 28 NFL teams against
the run. But this year, they gave up fewer
points than any other team! They also forced
43 turnovers, tops in the league.

After edging the Steelers, the Broncos destroyed the Cleveland Browns 37-21 . Elway
was brilliant, connecting on 26 of 30 passes
for 385 yards and three TDs. But the 49ers
were on a roll too. Playing their first season
under new coach George Seifert, who replaced
coaching legend Bill Walsh, the 49ers
trampled the tough Minnesota Vikings 41-13
in the first round of the play-offs. Then in the
NFC championship game, they stuffed the
Rams, a team many people thought was ready
to challenge the 'Niners. Montana was at his
best in the 30-3 victory, completing 26 of 30
passes for 262 yards and two touchdowns.
They outgained the Rams 442 yards to 156.
San Francisco looked unstoppable.

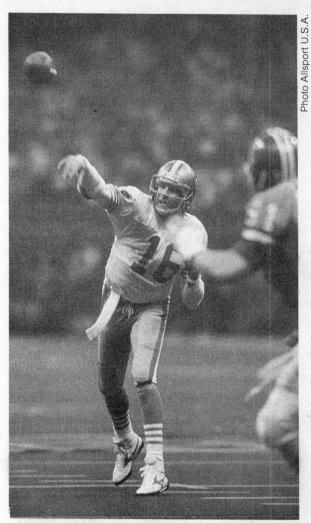

"Super" Joe Montana picks apart the Denver defense in the 55-10 blowout.

If any team *could* stop them, maybe it was the team that *had* stopped them. The Broncos were the only team that the 49ers hadn't beaten in the 1980s. Denver had beaten them three times in a row on late field goals. Over 70,000 revved-up fans packed the Superdome in New Orleans, expecting a high-scoring shootout. As it turned out, they were half-right.

Denver won the coin toss and elected to receive. Elway started firing away. He threw low. He threw high. He threw wide. Denver punted.

It was Montana's turn next. In contrast to Elway, he was crisp and efficient. Starting on their own 34-yard line, the 49ers scored 10 plays later when ace receiver Jerry Rice caught a Montana pass, bounced off a tackler, and sped into the end zone. San Francisco had the early lead, 7-0.

Rice was sending a message to the Broncos. "One thing about our receivers today," he said later, "was that we made up our minds we were not going to go down on the first hit. No matter what, we were going downfield."

The Broncos struck back on their next possession, narrowing the gap on a David Treadwell field goal. The highlight of the drive was a 27-yard Elway shuffle pass to running back Bobby Humphrey. And when Denver stopped the 49ers cold on the next series, fans were licking their chops at the prospect of a competitive matchup.

But on the very next play, Humphrey bobbled the ball at midfield, and San Francisco recovered. Montana led his team on a 10-play drive that ended with a TD toss to tight end Brent Jones. The missed extra point left the score at 13-6.

Elway kept misfiring. In Denver's first possession of the second quarter, Elway was nearly picked off twice. When the 49ers got the ball back, they went to the thundering ground attack of Tom Rathman and Roger Craig. Rathman scored the TD to put San Francisco on top 20-3.

Denver tried again. Elway, who had only connected on 2 of 11 throws so far, threw a perfect pass to Mark Jackson on third-and-11. But Jackson dropped the ball. When the 'Niners got the ball back, it took Montana only 64 seconds and five plays to go 59 yards. When Jerry Rice pulled in Montana's 38-yard pass for the score, fans felt the game was over. With a 27-3 lead going into the locker room, they started to wonder how many records the 49ers were going to set.

But on San Francisco's first possession, the Broncos stopped them. Were things looking up for Denver? No. With linebacker Charles

Haley in his face, Elway drilled a pass right into the hands of 49er Mike Walter. Montana and Rice teamed up immediately on another scoring pass and Cofer's PAT made it 34-3. And when Elway completed another pass— to another 49er—Montana added a 35-yard TD bomb to wideout John Taylor. It was 41-3, San Francisco!

The Broncos finally crossed the goal line on a 3-yard scoot by Elway. But the 49ers weren't through. A 75-yard, 11-play drive ended with a 4-yard Rathman TD run. The slaughter was up to 48-10.

When Elway was sacked and then fumbled the ball at the Denver 1-yard line, 49er linebacker Matt Millen tried to make him feel better. "Hang in there, it's a tough one," he said. "You got that right," Elway answered. After the 'Niner recovery, Rathman took it in to end the scoring. It was 55-10.

With 11 minutes left, Montana took a seat on the bench, and backup Steve Young came in to run the team. When the game ended, the 49ers had won their second straight Super Bowl. Their 55 points were a record, as was their 45-point margin. Their eight TDs also shattered a record.

Joe Montana was outstanding. He was the unanimous choice for MVP, his third. No other player had won it more than twice. He hit on

22 of 29 passes for 297 yards and no interceptions. His five touchdown passes were a record, as were Jerry Rice's three TD grabs. At one point, Montana hit 13 passes in a row—another record.

"The guy was awesome," marveled Elway later. "The whole offense was awesome."

Even the 49ers were impressed with their victory. Safety Ronnie Lott, who had played on all four San Francisco championship teams, said, "I knew we were great, but I didn't think we were going to be this great. No question, this is the most talented 49ers team that I've been on."

"We can now be mentioned in the same breath as the great teams like the Green Bay Packers and Pittsburgh Steelers and Miami Dolphins," added Jerry Rice.

In the losers' locker room, many Broncos were embarrassed. John Elway, who completed only 10 of 26 passes for 108 yards, two interceptions, four sacks, and a fumble, took the defeat hard. "You start questioning why we can't play better in this game," said the dejected QB. "We've played so poorly the three times I've been out there. We've just got to figure out how to win one of these things."

The win was especially sweet for new 'Niner head coach George Seifert, defensive coach under Bill Walsh. Never before had a rookie coach steered his team to a Super Bowl championship.

Were the 49ers the best team ever? With their performance in Super Bowl XXIV, they made a lot of believers!

SF	13	14	14	14	— 55
Denver	3	0	7	0	— 10

SF — Rice 20 pass from Montana (Cofer kick)

Denver — FG Treadwell 42

SF — Jones 7 pass from Montana (kick failed)

SF — Rathman 1 run (Cofer Kick)

SF — Rice 38 pass from Montana (Cofer kick)

SF — Rice 28 pass from Montana (Cofer kick)

SF — Taylor 35 pass from Montana (Cofer kick)

Denver — Elway 3 run (Treadwell kick)

SF — Rathman 4 run (Cofer kick)

SF — Craig 1 run (Cofer kick)

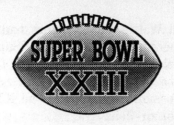

SUPER BOWL XXIII

CINCINNATI vs. SAN FRANCISCO

Joe Montana went into Super Bowl XXIII feeling he had something to prove.

In the 49ers' play-off loss to the Minnesota Vikings that ended the previous season, coach Bill Walsh had benched Montana in favor of backup Steve Young. Joe Montana was worried about losing his job.

In the 1989 season, both Montana and the 49ers had gotten off to a slow start. Montana's nagging injuries—sore back, sore shoulder, swollen elbow—had people talking about his age. His passes didn't have the same zip. Then Walsh rested Montana for a couple of games in the middle of the season for "fatigue." People were starting to whisper that maybe Montana was washed up at 32.

But Montana soon showed that there was a little magic left in his arm. He guided San Francisco to victories in four of the team's last five games, as the team ended up 10-6. But

Montana and the 49ers turned it up a notch in the play-offs, trouncing the Vikings 34-9. Then, in the bitter wind and cold of Chicago, Montana completed 17 of 27 passes for 288 yards. He lofted three beautiful TD passes as the 'Niners cruised 28-3.

For the Cincinnati Bengals, just reaching the Super Bowl was remarkable.

They'd been pretty awful the year before, winning four games and losing eleven. But with a spectacular season from their AFC Pro-Bowl quarterback Boomer Esiason, the Bengals had turned it around in a big way. Esiason threw for an astounding 3,572 yards and 28 TDs. Rookie running back sensation Ickey Woods rambled for 1,066 yards. The Bengals' record of 12-4 was the fourth best one-year turnaround in NFL history.

Cincy stormed through the play-offs. Their running game, best in the league, led them to a win over Seattle. By halftime, the rushing statistics read Bengals 165, Seahawks 0! In the AFC title game, the Bengals' massive offensive line, led by All-Pro tackle Anthony Munoz, ran over the Buffalo Bills 21-10.

Still, few people gave the Bengals much of a chance. In the last four Super Bowls, the NFC team had destroyed the AFC team.

But with running backs Woods and James Brooks and wide receiver Eddie Brown having great years, the Bengals had the league's most feared offense. Fans felt that the Bengals could hold their own against the 'Niners' balanced attack. But there was a big edge to the 49er defense.

Also, Cincinnati fans had something else to worry about—the late-season decline in Boomer Esiason's passing numbers. There were rumors that a late-season sprain of the index finger on his throwing hand had left him unable to grip the ball well enough. But the big southpaw was tough. He had once played the whole second half of a college game with a separated shoulder.

Then, at the 49ers' workout on the Monday before the game, there was news that sent the Cincy fans' hopes soaring. It plunged the 49er fans into a panic. Jerry Rice, the greatest receiver in the league, twisted his ankle, had to skip three practices, and was limping badly.

But just hours before the 75,179 fans surged into Miami's Joe Robbie Stadium, the Bengal fans were hit with their own shocker. Running back Stanley Wilson, who had had two previous suspensions, was once again found with cocaine. His career was over.

The news hit many Bengal players hard. They were worried about how their teammate would rescue his life. "Everyone tried to shake it off, but the mood wasn't the same," admitted cornerback Lewis Billups.

And so the stage was set for Super Bowl XXIII, a rematch of Super Bowl XVI. The 49ers won that one—and the Bengals wanted revenge.

San Francisco won the toss and chose to receive. On the third play of the game, their offensive tackle Steve Wallace was carried off the field with a broken leg. On the last play of the series, Montana fumbled the snap and had to fall on the ball. It wasn't the best of beginnings.

After the Bengals had to punt, San Francisco started from their own 3. On the very first play of the 'Niner drive, Cincinnati's Pro-Bowl nose tackle Tim Krumrie became the game's second victim. He shattered both major bones in his left leg. "He's the centerpiece of our defense. When we lost him, we lost our best tackler," lamented Bengal coach Sam Wyche.

San Francisco was first on the scoreboard. A 15-yard penalty for a late hit on Montana and a key third-down conversion by Tom Rathman got the 49ers into field-goal range. Mike Cofer's 41-yarder sailed through the uprights for a 3-0 lead.

The 49ers then blew three scoring opportunities. First, safety Ronnie Lott missed a golden chance for an interception at the

Bengal 40-yard line. On the 49ers' next possession, Randy Cross's low snap forced Cofer's two-yard FG attempt to miss left. Then John Taylor's sensational 45-yard punt return, longest in Super Bowl history, gave the team excellent field position at the Bengal 46. The drive fell apart as the 49ers fumbled.

Starting off in San Francisco territory near the end of the first half, the Bengals were finally able to capitalize on the 49er mistakes. Placekicker Jim Breech knotted the game at 3-3 with a 34-yarder.

Blitzed and pressured throughout the half, Boomer Esiason underthrew his receivers and overthrew his receivers. He hit them only 4 of 12 times for a measly 48 yards. Montana was 9-16 for 114 yards. San Francisco picked up 23 first downs to only 13 for Cincy. The 49ers had completely outplayed the Bengals in the first half. But they could only manage a 3-3 tie.

The action heated up in a hurry as the second half began. Esiason marched his team down the field. The Bengal drive lasted 13 plays, gained 61 yards, and ate 9:21 off the clock. Jim Breech finished it off with a 43-yard field goal to give the Bengals a 6-3 lead. Breech had only made two FGs longer than 40 yards all year, but he was on the money this time.

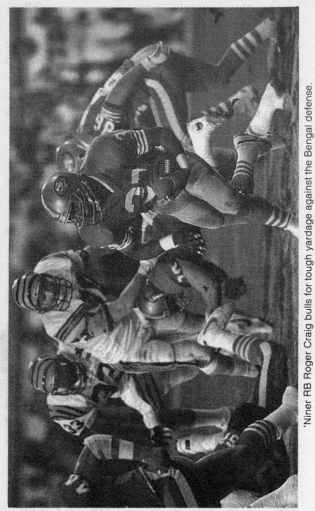

'Niner RB Roger Craig bulls for tough yardage against the Bengal defense.

On the Bengals' next possession, 'Niner linebacker Jim Romanowski picked off an Esiason pass, giving San Francisco the ball at the Bengal 23-yard line. Cincinnati looked to be in real trouble. But the Bengal defense proved fierce. They refused to yield even a first down, forcing the 49ers to settle for another Mike Cofer field goal. The score was knotted again, 6-6.

When Cofer kicked off, Bengal return specialist Stanford Jennings brought the crowd to their feet with the game's most spectacular play: a 93-yard run up the middle all the way to the end zone. Suddenly, the Bengals had a 13-6 lead over the mighty 49ers.

With just 34 seconds remaining in the third quarter, trailing by seven, San Francisco had the ball on its own 15-yard line. It didn't take long for Montana to pull another comeback out of his bag of tricks. He went straight to work. It only took four plays to cover the 85 yards. He hit Rice for 31 and running back Roger Craig for 40. Then the Bengals' rookie cornerback, Lewis Billups, had a chance to be a hero. Montana fired a pass into the end zone for John Taylor. Billups was able to break up the pass. But he dropped the ball, losing the possible interception.

Then it was Jerry Rice's turn for some heroics. Running an out pattern, he got away from Billups, snagged Montana's pass at the 5, and, with Billups trying to shove him out of bounds, lunged for the end zone. He stretched his right hand, which was cradling the ball, out over the corner of the end zone, just over the goal line, as he was tumbling out of bounds. The ref ruled touchdown! Cofer's PAT tied the score again. "I had never dived into the end zone like that in my life; so I'll remember that one," said Rice after the game.

The game, which had been billed as a matchup of two great offenses, had gone 44 minutes, 26 seconds without a touchdown, a Super Bowl record. Then, like lightning, the two teams scored two TDs in 91 seconds!

On their first possession of the fourth quarter, the Bengals failed to score. Montana had the 'Niners on the move again. Rice, who had thrilled fans all game with his incredible catches, was at it again. Racing step for step downfield with Lewis Billups, Rice soared high into the air to snare another Montana bomb. He re-twisted his hurt ankle on the 44-yard gain. But the catch was wasted when Cofer missed a 49-yard field goal attempt.

Then the Bengals' number-one offense began to fire on all cylinders. Taking over on his own 32, Esiason moved his team 46 yards in 11 plays. Jim Breech's 40-yard field goal gave Cincy a 16-13 lead with just 3:20 to play.

Could the outmanned Bengal defense make the lead stand up against the offensive onslaught that they knew was coming? Fans around the world held their breath and watched.

Excitement was in the air as the 49ers got the ball back for a final try. The lead had shifted back and forth throughout the whole game. Everything was riding on this drive. Was there any more magic left in the quarterback's bag?

When a holding penalty on the kickoff shoved the 49ers back to their 8-yard line, things looked dark for San Francisco. They were 92 yards from victory. But Montana, cool as usual, went to work, hitting Roger Craig, tight end John Frank, and Jerry Rice up the middle on three straight completions. Two Craig runs, also up the middle, set up the Bengal defense for a switch to sideline passes to stop the clock. Rice outdistanced Billups on the left for 17 yards to cross midfield. A 13-yard toss to Craig along the right sideline took the 'Niners to the Bengal 35.

The excitement reached fever pitch. Joe Montana, screaming out plays, began to hyperventilate. Afraid that his wooziness might cause him to throw an interception, he threw the ball way out of bounds to buy some time.

The 49er drive almost screeched to a halt on the next play. Center Randy Cross got caught too far upfield on a pass play. The yellow flag flew. The ineligible-receiver-downfield penalty broke the momentum and pushed the 49ers back to the Bengal 45—out of field-goal range. But it was Jerry Rice to the rescue, gimpy ankle and all. Eluding three defenders, he hauled in a 27-yard throw that moved the 49ers to the Bengal 18.

A field goal would have tied the score. But the 'Niners went for the kill. A pass to Craig took the ball down to the 10-yard line with 39 seconds to go. Montana called a time out. It was for all the marbles now.

Craig, the primary receiver, circled out of the backfield to the right, drawing double coverage. Rice went in motion to the left, also attracting two defenders. That left John Taylor open in the middle. Montana's pass was dead on the money, and the heart of every Bengal fan broke at the same time. Taylor was in the end zone. And the legend of Super Joe Montana was carved in the memory of every football fan. From now on, football fans would refer to the end of Super Bowl XXIII simply as The Drive.

"We were 34 seconds away from a glorious victory," said a dejected Boomer Esiason after the game. "It's a very empty feeling. When you come so close to the top of the mountain and lose it this way, it really hurts."

The 49ers were champions for the third time in the decade of the 1980s. The game had held a lot of surprises. The Bengals' vaunted no-huddle offense, expected to explode for big yardage, never really got untracked. Ickey Woods gained 79 yards, but never got to do his famous TD dance, the Ickey Shuffle. Boomer Esiason struggled, completing only 11 of 25 passes for 144 yards and no touchdowns. He was sacked five times. But the Bengal defense, ranked 15th in the NFL and criticized all year, came through when it counted. The defense's valiant effort kept the game close to the very end, even though the 49ers outgained the Bengals in total yardage 454 to 229. Bengal fans couldn't help wondering what might have happened if the anchor of their defense, Tim Krumrie, had been able to play. They would never know if Montana could have engineered The Drive with Krumrie in his face.

And Jerry Rice, who dazzled the fans with 11 catches for a record-breaking 215 yards and one TD—all on a sprained ankle—took home the MVP award. But in both the winning and losing locker rooms, it was Joe Montana who got most of the praise. "All the time we were confident we could score," said a jubilant

Randy Cross of the 49ers. "Joe handles situations like that better than anyone who's ever played the game."

Bengal receiver Chris Collinsworth marveled, too. "Joe Montana is not human," he said. "I don't want to call him a god, but he's definitely somewhere in between."

```
Cincinnati   0   3   10   3 — 16
S. F.        3   0    3 14 — 20
```

SF —FG Cofer 41
Cin—FG Breech 34
Cin—FG Breech 43
SF —FG Cofer 32
Cin—Jennings 93 kickoff return (Breech kick)
SF —Rice 14 pass from Montana (Cofer kick)
Cin—FG Breech 40
SF —Taylor 10 pass from Montana
      (Cofer kick)

SUPER BOWL XXII

WASHINGTON vs. DENVER

In the days before any Super Bowl, football fans always argue about the quarterback match-up. Going into Super Bowl XXII, however, the quarterback match-up seemed like no contest at all.

On one side stood Denver's Golden Boy John Elway, one of the top quarterbacks in the NFL. He entered Super Bowl XXII after an outstanding regular season and a great play-off performance. And his fans expected more of the same in the Super Bowl.

On the other side stood Washington's Doug Williams. Williams had not even played in half of the Redskins' games during the 1987 season. And in the play-off games, Williams had performed unevenly. It seemed as if he played only well enough to pull out the victories. Few football experts expected much from him in the big game. Some even suggested he was the type of player who crumbles under pressure.

Williams, who had played pro football for nine years, was used to people saying these kinds of things about him. He had certainly seen more of the down side of the NFL than the up side. His career started strongly enough. He was the first draft choice of the Tampa Bay Buccaneers in 1978. Williams went on to win all-rookie-team honors that year. In the very next season, he led the Bucs to their first NFC Central title. Williams helped the Bucs earn two more play-off spots in the next three seasons.

But then he and team management failed to agree on a contract before the 1983 season. So he decided to play for the Oklahoma Outlaws, who were part of the old United States Football League (USFL). This change meant he had to sit out the 1983 season.

Williams had a couple of decent seasons in the USFL after that. But the league got so little attention that Williams nearly disappeared from the public eye. When the USFL folded, Williams was free to return to the NFL. The Washington Redskins signed him on as a backup to their young star Jay Schroeder. But by the 1987 season opener, the cannon-armed Williams was neck-to-neck with Schroeder for the starting quarterback position.

Because of his bumpy career, the 32-year-old Williams wasn't exactly a household name. In fact, his main claim to fame coming into Super Bowl XXII was that he would become the first black quarterback to start a Super Bowl game. But Williams himself didn't want the pregame focus to rest on his color. "Coach Joe Gibbs did not bring me in to be the first black quarterback in the Super Bowl," said Williams. "He brought me in to be the quarterback of the Washington Redskins."

Williams was low-key about his importance on the team. "I don't have to play well for us to win," he said before the game. "What I have to do is not beat the Redskins by throwing interceptions or turning the ball over."

And so Doug Williams remained in the shadow of Denver quarterback John Elway. Elway, after all, was expected to play a great game against the Washington Redskins. The Denver fans believed Elway could carry his team all by himself if he had to. But they didn't think he'd have to.

Elway and the Broncos finished the strike-shortened 1987 season with a 10-4-1 record. The "Big Orange," as the Broncos were called, dominated the AFC by winning six of their final seven games. Denver opened the play-offs with a 34-10 win over Houston. Then, in the AFC championship game, Denver won another exciting victory over the Cleveland Browns 38-33.

The Redskins had an 11-4 record during the 1987 season. They had been in danger of losing their season-ending game to Minnesota with Schroeder as the starting quarterback. Then Williams stepped in and led Washington to a come-from-behind victory in OT. That earned Doug the starting nod in the play-offs.

Williams guided the 'Skins to a 21-17 victory over the Chicago Bears. The Redskins again met the Vikings, this time for the NFC title. Washington won a classic defensive struggle 17-10, to earn a Bowl trip.

This was to be Denver's second straight Super Bowl game and third overall. The Broncos had lost the year before to the New York Giants. Washington was playing in the big one for the fourth time. They had won once and lost twice in their Super Bowl history. Oddsmakers favored the Broncos by 3-1/2 points, because of their recent Super Bowl experience and because of John Elway's passing arm.

More than 73,000 fans packed San Diego's Jack Murphy Stadium. The weather—sunny and warm—was perfect for football, but the field was soggy and slippery in places. So the players each brought along several pairs of shoes to see what would work best.

Most people expected a high-scoring game, right from the start. So it was something of a let-down when Washington went nowhere on its first possession. A short punt gave Denver the ball at its own 44-yard line.

The Denver offense set up in the shotgun, a passing formation. Elway took the snap and went for the bomb right away. The ball soared 30...40...50...60...70 yards in the air and landed in the outstretched arms of wide receiver Ricky Nattiel. Nattiel cradled the pass at the 5-yard line and scampered into the end zone. Touchdown, Denver!

The 56-yard TD play electrified the crowd! It was the earliest touchdown in Super Bowl history. Only 1:57 had elapsed in the game. And rookie Ricky Nattiel became the youngest player ever to score in the Super Bowl. Rich Karlis kicked the extra point to give Denver a startling 7-0 lead.

Elway later recalled the Denver mood after that sudden TD strike. "We felt good," said Elway. "We felt coming in we had a lot of confidence in our offense. We wanted to come out and take a chance on the big play. That got us going."

'Skins defensive back Barry Wilburn, who was burned on the Nattiel catch, had a different viewpoint. "They woke me up early," said Wilburn. "They caught me off guard and made the big play. I knew I wasn't going to let that happen again."

Denver's defense, inspired by the quick score, stopped Washington's next drive after five plays. Denver took over at its own 32-yard line after the punt.

Elway again drove the Broncos down the field. He passed 32 yards to wide receiver Mark Jackson. On a trick play, Elway actually caught a 23-yard pass from running back Steve Sewell. Elway became the first quarterback in Super Bowl history to *catch* a pass! Denver's drive stalled at the Washington 7-yard line. Rich Karlis booted a 24-yard field goal. Denver led 10-0 with less than six minutes gone in the opening quarter.

History was now on Denver's side. No team had ever come back from more than a seven-point deficit to win a Super Bowl game.

The Broncos very nearly wrapped up the game on the next kickoff. Washington return ace Ricky Sanders fumbled the ball after a hard Denver hit. The ball disappeared in a huge pile-up. Somehow, Redskins linebacker Ravin Caldwell managed to come up with the loose pigskin. A Denver recovery might have put a quick lock on Super Bowl XXII.

But the 'Skins' recovered fumble gave Washington's defensive players time to take a deep breath and to do some thinking.

Denver's speedy offensive players had left the 'Skins slipping and sliding on the loose turf. The Redskins decided to change shoes. They hoped that the longer cleats on the new shoes would give them better traction.

It was the right choice. Denver's next drive was crushed when the Redskins sacked John Elway. But after getting the ball back, near-disaster struck the Washington offense. Doug Williams dropped deep to pass. He tried to plant his right foot, but it slid right out from under him. As he fell, he twisted his left knee. Williams slowly rose up to return to the huddle. He wobbled and then collapsed to the ground. Doug Williams had to be helped off the field. And with him went the hopes of millions of Redskin fans.

"When I saw him go down again, I thought 'Uh-oh, something's wrong,'" said Washington trainer Bubba Tyler. "It (his left knee) was stretched—hyperflexed, we call it. I taped it and put a brace over it."

Jay Schroeder replaced Williams for a couple of plays. Then Washington turned the ball back over to Denver. Once again, the Broncos could not move against the Redskins. The second quarter began with Denver ahead 10-0. But the Broncos soon had to punt the ball to Washington. The 'Skins took over at their own 20-yard line.

And then the fans saw an amazing sight. Doug Williams, with his knee in a brace, trotted gingerly back onto the field. He looked pretty shaky. Most spectators thought he would hand off a couple of times to test his knee. But Williams had other ideas. His other ideas would lead to the most amazing quarter of football ever seen in a Super Bowl.

He took a straight drop from center. He didn't even fake a hand-off. This was a pass play all the way. Williams planted his foot to pass. This time he didn't slip. He lofted a soft spiral down the right sideline. Wide receiver Ricky Sanders streaked under the ball and caught it near midfield. He raced untouched down the sidelines for an 80-yard touchdown play. Ali Haji-Sheikh kicked the extra point. In just 53 seconds of the second quarter, the 'Skins had cut Denver's lead to 10-7.

The 80-yard Williams-to-Sanders play tied a Super Bowl record for the longest passing play. Even more important, the touchdown gave the Redskins their first ray of hope in Super Bowl XXII. And quarterback Doug Williams seemed to be back in top form. His knee had to be hurting, but he wasn't showing it.

"That was the lift we needed," said Washington coach Joe Gibbs. "I think it was then we all said, 'Hey, we're back on track.' "

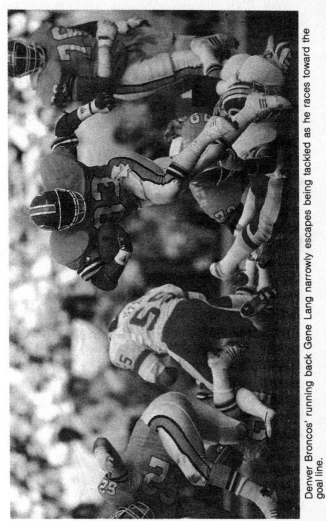

Denver Broncos' running back Gene Lang narrowly escapes being tackled as he races toward the goal line.

Washington's tough defense held Denver on three downs and forced a punt. Williams and the offense had the ball right back at their own 36-yard line. "We could tell something was in the works, something was happening," said 'Skins defensive tackle Dave Butz.

The long TD pass had loosened up Denver's defense. So Doug Williams cranked up the Washington running game. He sent rookie running back Timmy Smith through the left side for 19 yards. Then he passed 9 yards to Don Warren. In four plays, the 'Skins had moved to Denver's 27-yard line.

Williams again took a straight drop and set to pass. Wide receiver Gary Clark, who had already dropped two passes, faked inside and cut outside. Williams lofted a pass down the left side. The ball headed in an arc toward the goal line. Clark reached, grabbed the ball, dived to the ground and rolled into the end zone. Touchdown, Washington! Haji-Sheikh's kick gave the Redskins a 14-10 lead with 4:45 gone in the second period.

"I knew 10 points would not win the game," said Williams afterward.

Elway and the Broncos, behind for the first time, put another solid drive together. Elway moved his offense to Washington's 26-yard line before the 'Skins stopped him. But Rich Karlis missed a 43-yard field goal.

So Washington got the ball back at its 26-yard line. Williams snaked a pass over the middle. Gary Clark pulled it in for a 16-yard gain. On the next snap, Williams delayed a beat and then handed off to Timmy Smith. Smith exploded untouched through the right side of the line. Only safety Tony Lilly stood between Smith and the goal line. Lilly didn't have a chance. Smith raced 58 yards! Haji-Sheikh kicked the extra point. Washington now led 21-10. And the second quarter was only half over. The Broncos were in a state of shock. But the Redskins weren't finished.

Denver ran three plays and punted. Williams went to work at his own 40-yard line. He passed to Ricky Sanders for 10 yards. Then Williams faked a hand off to Smith and dropped back to pass. Sanders ran from the left side of the field deep into the right corner. Williams fired the ball downfield. Sanders snagged the pass at the 7-yard line and ran into the end zone. The 50-yard TD play was Sanders' second score of the period. Haji-Sheikh kicked another extra point. With four minutes left in the first half, Washington led 28-10.

The shell-shocked Denver Broncos tried to make a game of it. But Elway, dogged by Dexter Manley and Charles Mann, threw wildly. His pass was intercepted by defensive back Barry Wilburn.

Williams and the 'Skins started at their own 21-yard line this time. They seemed content to stay on the ground and run out the clock. A 28-10 lead was, after all, a big edge at halftime. But Washington's offensive line wasn't finished yet! Timmy Smith roared through a huge hole in Denver's sagging defense for a gain of 43 yards.

Williams took advantage of the scoring opportunity provided by Smith. He drove the offense quickly down to Denver's 8-yard line. Then he hit tight end Clint Didier deep in the left corner of the end zone for still another touchdown. Haji-Sheikh's kick made the score 35-10. Denver's final first-half possession ended in another interception.

Halftime gave the players and fans a breather from the incredible Redskin offensive onslaught. It also gave the statisticians time to check the record book.

Washington's five second-quarter TDs broke the old record of three in a quarter. The 'Skins' 356 yards of total offense in that period set an all-time NFL play-off record. And those play-off records go back some 60 years. Some say it was the most yardage of any quarter in *any* NFL game, but that will never be proven. Those kinds of statistics were not kept early in NFL history.

Williams himself tied a Super Bowl record with four TD passes. Terry Bradshaw of the Pittsburgh Steelers had thrown four in a whole game. Williams completed 9 of 11 passes for 228 yards in one period.

Denver's four second-half drives ended in punts and frustration. Behind by so many points, Elway had to pass again and again. Washington's defensive linemen chased after Elway on nearly every play. The 'Skins sacked Elway five times and forced many bad passes.

Washington's offense, in the meantime, continued to run up yardage and points and records. Timmy Smith ran the ball time after time on the same off-tackle play. He racked up big chunks of yardage almost every time. Early in the fourth quarter, he raced for a 32-yard gain. Then he took it in from four yards out for Washington's final TD. It was Smith's second TD of the game—the only two touchdowns in his young NFL career! Washington led 42-10. And that's how it ended.

More records fell. Timmy Smith gained a record 204 rushing yards on 22 carries. Doug Williams finished with 18-of-29 passing for a record 340 yards. Ricky Sanders ended up with 9 receptions for a record 193 yards receiving. And the Redskins as a team gained 602 yards, another Super Bowl record.

But among all those record-setters, it was

underdog Doug Williams who stood out. Battered and bruised, he led the Redskins to the greatest quarter in NFL play-off history. And he led his team to a lopsided Super Bowl victory. For his performance, Doug Williams was the unanimous choice as MVP.

Elway finished with 257 yards passing. "We've got to be a better football team," said Elway after it was over. "I don't think we're good enough to win the Super Bowl. We know how to get there. We've just got to find out how to win one.

"I know a lot of quarterbacks never get to the Super Bowl," Elway continued. "In my career, the ultimate is to win this game. I will not have a good feeling about myself until I win one."

Doug Williams could understand Elway's overwhelming desire to win. "I wanted to go out and perform up to my abilities and try to win the football game," Williams said. "I had some pain, but I just sucked it up."

"I'm proud of him in all ways, including being the first black quarterback and the way he handled himself," said offensive lineman Mark May. "He's a leader."

"It's a tribute not only to a black quarterback, but to a very great quarterback," said Redskins owner Jack Kent Cooke.

Coach Joe Gibbs knew it hadn't been easy

for Williams. "There was certainly a lot of pressure on him," he said. "He handled it extremely well."

"I really did not come here as a black quarterback," concluded Williams. "I came here as a quarterback for the Washington Redskins. I came here to win for the Redskins, and we did.

"I'm not some kind of experiment," added the Super Bowl MVP. "I'm a good quarterback. And I really don't think the football cares what color I am."

```
Washington  0   35  0   7   — 42
Denver      10   0  0   0   — 10
```

Den —Nattiel 56 pass from Elway
       (Karlis kick)
Den —FG Karlis 24
Wash—Sanders 80 pass from Williams
       (Haji-Sheikh kick)
Wash—G. Clark 27 pass from Williams
       (Haji-Sheikh kick)
Wash—T. Smith 58 run (Haji-Sheikh kick)
Wash—Sanders 50 pass from Williams
       (Haji-Sheikh kick)
Wash—Didier 8 pass from Williams
       (Haji-Sheikh kick)
Wash—T. Smith 4 run (Haji-Sheikh kick)

SUPER BOWL XXI

NEW YORK GIANTS vs. DENVER

Almost every football fan in America knew that the Denver Broncos didn't have much of a chance of winning Super Bowl XXI. People thought that the New York Giants, led by their awesome linebacking corps, were going to run away with the Super Bowl trophy.

But some Denver fans didn't think so. They were placing their hope on football history. They reminded Giants fans of Super Bowl III. At that Super Bowl, a brash young quarterback named Joe Namath became a household name. Namath led the Jets to the biggest upset in NFL history.

The Broncos had their own giant-killer in big blond bomb-thrower John Elway. The 6-foot-3, 210-pound fourth-year pro had become one of the top quarterbacks in the NFL. During the 1986 season he lead the Broncos to an 11-5 finish in the tough AFC West. Elway completed 280 of his 504 passes—a 55.6 completion percentage—in leading Denver to the division title. He tossed 19 touchdown passes during the regular season. And he suffered only 13 interceptions.

The Broncos edged the defending AFC champion New England Patriots, 22-17, to open the play-offs. Denver then met the Cleveland Browns in the AFC title game. The Browns led most of the way, holding a 20-13 lead late in the fourth quarter. Denver was pinned at its own 2-yard line and things looked hopeless. But Elway, who hadn't had the greatest of days, suddenly came alive. He completed pass after pass, including a crucial third-and-18 play for a first down. He scrambled for more yardage on his own. He inspired the Broncos to the tying touchdown with only seconds remaining. The game was tied at 20-20 and went into overtime. Then Elway commanded another big drive that led to the winning field goal.

The Broncos were in the Super Bowl! Many people considered Elway's late rally in the Cleveland victory to be the best performance by a quarterback in the entire 1986 NFL season.

If the Broncos were to win Super Bowl XXI, it would have to be on the slingshot arm of John Elway. Elway was going to have to score points against the best defense in the NFL in 1986. He was going to have to drive down the field against some of the best linebackers ever to play the game.

New York's Lawrence Taylor, Carl Banks, Harry Carson, and Gary Reasons were Goliaths on the gridiron. The smallest of the crew was Taylor, at 6-foot-3 and 237 pounds. These New York linebackers controlled every game the Giants won in 1986. They smashed the run. They crushed the quarterback. They covered receivers out of the backfield. They blasted and crashed and ruined perfectly good offenses. And if those four weren't enough, backups Andy Headen, Pepper Johnson, and Byron Hunt often subbed in key situations. These guys could have started for almost any other NFL team.

This gang of defenders led the Giants to the NFL's best record in 1986 at 14-2. One of those victories was over the Broncos 19-16. New York won the tough NFC East division title.

The Giants rammed their way through the play-offs. The defense set up countless opportunities for the offense. Quarterback Phil Simms and running back Joe Morris piled up the points. The Giants were awe-inspiring. They blasted the proud San Francisco 49ers 49-3. That game is best remembered for one particular play.

San Francisco's offensive line, so concerned about blitzing linebackers, left defensive tackle Jim Burt with a clear shot at QB Joe Montana. Burt, making a clean hit, knocked Montana unconscious. Then the Giants faced NFC East rival Washington for the NFC title. New York had already beaten Washington twice during the regular season. They made it three straight with a 17-0 whitewash. To the surprise of no one, the New York Giants were Super Bowl-bound.

The stage was set for Super Bowl XXI in the jam-packed Rose Bowl in Pasadena, California. The Giants entered the game as solid 9-point favorites. The huge crowd of 101,063 was dominated by fans in Giant blue who expected New York to run away with the game. John Elway, the David with the sling-shot arm, was ready to take on that Goliath linebacking corps of the Giants.

Elway and the Broncos started off with an impressive drive. Denver started at its own 24-yard line after the opening kickoff. Elway dropped back to pass, felt the heat from the blitzing linebackers, and scrambled 10 yards for a first down. A couple of short rushing plays followed. Then Elway hit rookie wide receiver Mark Jackson with a big 24-yard completion. But the drive stalled at New York's 31-yard line. Rich Karlis kicked a 48-

yard field goal to give Denver a 3-0 lead less than five minutes into the game. The kick tied the Super Bowl record for the longest field goal.

The Giants answered right back on their first possession. Quarterback Phil Simms passed on the first two plays from scrimmage. He hit Lionel Manuel for 17 yards and tight end Mark Bavaro for 9. Joe Morris then rambled around the right side for 11 yards. Two plays later Simms connected with Stacy Robinson on a pinpoint 18-yard sideline pass play. On second-and-10 from the Denver 23-yard line, Simms again fired a perfect pass. He hit tight end Bavaro for 17 yards up the middle. On first-and-goal from the 6, Simms zipped a pass to backup tight end Zeke Mowatt for the TD. Raul Allegre kicked the extra point. New York led 7-3, with five minutes left in the opening quarter. Phil Simms, who took a back seat to John Elway in all the pre-game talk, went six for six for 69 yards on the TD drive.

Elway rose to the challenge. A long kickoff return by Ken Bell gave Denver the ball at the 42-yard line. Elway immediately hit running back Sammy Winder for 13 yards in the left flat. Then he found tight end Orson Mobley for 11 yards on the right sideline. Winder took a screen pass for 9 yards up the middle. Linebacker Harry Carson hit Winder out of bounds and drew a personal foul penalty. A ticked-off Lawrence Taylor kicked the ref's flag. That cost another 15 yards. The Broncos were suddenly on New York's 6-yard line.

A running play lost three yards. Then Elway sizzled a 5-yard pass to Vance Johnson over the middle. On third-and-goal from the 4, Elway set up in the shotgun. He took the snap, delayed a moment, and ran a quarterback draw up the middle for the touchdown. Karlis kicked the extra point. The fans couldn't believe it. The Broncos held a 10-7 lead.

New York's ferocious defense hadn't stood out yet. The attention was on the two quarterbacks. Elway, to the surprise of few, had completed all six of his passes. To the surprise of many, so had Phil Simms. These signal-callers were fast becoming the story of Super Bowl XXI.

The Broncos got the ball back early in the second period. Elway drove the Denver offense down the field. He rolled right and threw across the field to a streaking Vance Johnson. The play was good for 54 yards. On another third-down play, Elway passed to Mobley for a first down. On still another third down, Elway hit running back Steve Sewell for a first-down completion. Sewell was then

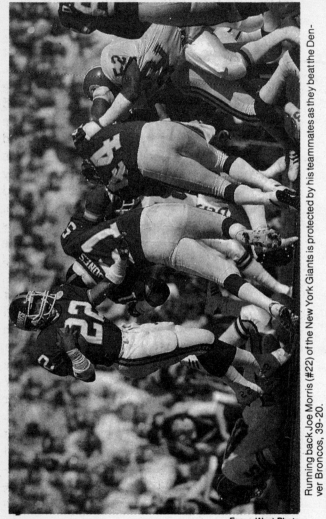

Running back Joe Morris (#22) of the New York Giants is protected by his teammates as they beat the Denver Broncos, 39-20.

Focus West Photo

tackled at the Giants' l-yard line.

The Broncos had the opportunity of a life-time! A touchdown now would mean a 17-7 lead over the mighty Giants. Elway swept right on first down. He lost two yards. Running back Gerald Willhite crashed up the middle. He was met by Harry Carson and crunched for no gain. On third-and-goal from the 3, Sammy Winder took a pitch-out and headed around the left side. Harry Carson took Winder down for a 3-yard loss, wrapping up a brilliant goal line stand. Denver head coach Dan Reeves sent out the field goal team. But the usually dependable Rich Karlis hooked the kick wide to the right. It was the shortest missed field goal in Super Bowl history.

Denver's defense held, and the Broncos got the ball back. Defensive end Leonard Marshall sacked Elway on first down. Then Elway passed to tight end Clarence Kay for what appeared to be a first down. But one official ruled the pass incomplete. A TV replay followed, the first one ever in a Super Bowl. No clearcut replay angle could be found. The play was ruled incomplete. On the next play, Elway set up to pass. The Giants put on a tremendous pass rush. Veteran defensive end George Martin sacked Elway in the end zone for a safety. The lead was cut down

to 10-9 with 2:46 left in the half. New York's
defensive might was starting to show.

Unluckily for the Broncos, a later replay
showed that Clarence Kay's catch was good.
But it was too late. The safety stood. The
momentum was changing.

Denver did get one more chance in the first
half. Elway passed brilliantly to wide receiver
Steve Watson for 31 yards on the right sideline. Then he shoveled a pass to Willhite for
11 more yards. The Broncos had a first down
at the New York 21-yard line with less than
a minute left. Elway, under pressure, misfired
on three straight pass attempts. An offsides
penalty on the Giants moved the ball down
to the 16. On fourth down, Karlis came in for
a 34-yard field goal. Once again, he missed to
the right.

The half ended at 10-9. And even though
Denver still had a one-point lead, the momentum had moved over to the Giants. By miss-
ing opportunities, the Broncos were killing
themselves. New York's defense was coming
on strong! And New York's Phil Simms, un-
expectedly, was having the greatest game of
his career.

New York head coach Bill Parcells later
recalled his halftime speech. " 'Hey, let's don't
give the game away,'" I said. 'I don't mind
getting beat, but I don't want to come this

far and give it away.' I talked about playing with more discipline. I told them Elway would complete some passes, but to forget them and get up and get the guys the next time."

The Giants did come out and "get the guys" in the third quarter. The way the game turned from nail-biter to rout was enough to make your head spin!.

New York took the second half kickoff, but their drive stalled at their own 46-yard line, fourth-and-one. Parcells sent out the punting team, with backup quarterback Jeff Rutledge as the short man in the formation. Suddenly Rutledge moved to the quarterback spot. He took the snap and dived into a small hole for the first down. The gamble on the fake punt paid off.

With the drive still alive, Simms passed 12 yards to Joe Morris in the right flat. He passed 23 yards to Lee Rouson on the left side. On third-and-six from the Denver 13-yard line, Simms found Bavaro up the middle. He fired a perfect pass into double coverage for the touchdown. Allegre's kick gave New York a 16-10 lead.

The teams exchanged a series of punts before New York got the ball back late in the third period. A pair of runs by Morris and a pass by Simms to Lionel Manuel moved the ball to Denver's 45. Simms again handed off to Morris. But this was to be no normal running play. Morris turned and lateraled back to Sims. The quarterback then lofted a long sideline pass to wide-open McConkey. The speedy wide receiver was not pulled down until he reached the 1-yard line. Morris went over right tackle for the TD. Allegre kicked the extra point. New York led 26-10 with 24 seconds left in the third quarter.

Early in the fourth quarter, the Giants made Elway pay for a big mistake. Elway winged a pass for Mark Jackson, but Elvis Patterson stepped in and picked it off. Seven plays later, the Giants rolled in for an insurance TD. Simms fired a pass to tight end Mark Bavaro. Bavaro tipped the ball, and it fell right into the hands of a surprised Phil McConkey for the TD. Allegre's extra point made it 33-10.

Elway completed five of six passes on Denver's next possession. But the Broncos had to settle for a field goal when they desperately needed a TD. The score moved to 33-13. New York recovered Denver's onside kick at the Bronco 46. Simms drove the Giants down the field. He bootlegged 22 yards for a big first down. From the 2-yard line, Simms sent veteran running back Ottis Anderson up the middle for another TD. Allegre's extra point try flew wide left. New York upped its lead to 39-13.

Elway led the Broncos on another scoring drive late in the game. He hit a streaking Vance Johnson up the middle for a 53-yard TD bomb. Karlis connected on the extra point kick and New York's lead was 39-20.

Simms sat out the rest of the game, letting Jeff Rutledge play. Simms completed all 10 of his second half passes en route to 22 completions in 25 attempts on the day. He threw for 268 yards, three touchdowns, and no interceptions. His 88 percent completion percentage was by far a Super Bowl record.

The gun sounded. New York's 39-20 victory was history. Within seconds it was announced that Phil Simms was the game's MVP. After all the talk of John Elway and the Giant linebackers, it was Simms who stole the show.

"I don't think Phil threw one bad pass," said New York coach Parcells. "He played about as well as you can play. He was magnificent. He had control of the game throughout. I am happy for Phil Simms."

The superb New York linebackers picked up 28 of the team's 49 tackles on the day. Carl Banks led the way with 10 solo tackles. But it was all-world linebacker Lawrence Taylor who spoke for the squad.

"As long as I live, I'll always have a Super Bowl ring," said a jubilant Taylor. "One time in my career we were considered the best in the world. That's the most important thing."

Nearly lost in the celebration was the magnificent performance by John Elway in the losing cause. The Denver quarterback completed 22 of 27 passes for 304 yards. He became only the fifth Super Bowl quarterback ever to go over 300 yards. Elway was also Denver's leading rusher for the game with only 27 yards.

Perhaps no Bronco took the defeat worse than kicker Rich Karlis. His missed field goals in the second quarter would haunt him forever. "The kicks meant so much," said a tearful Karlis in the losers' locker room. "I let the momentum swing. I thought about all the people I let down, all the guys who put their hearts and souls into this game. Right now, I'm hurting. I apologize."

But linebacker Karl Mecklenburg defended his teammate. "The way the Giants moved the ball in the second half, six points wouldn't have made a difference," admitted the all-pro linebacker.

Now it was official—the Giants were the best. Not even John Elway, the giant-killer, could prevent these Goliaths from stomping off with the Vince Lombardi trophy for Super Bowl XXI.

```
Denver     0  0   0 10 — 20
New York   7  2  17 13 — 39
```

Den—FG Karlis 48
NY —Mowatt 6 pass from Simms
      (Allegre kick)
Den—Elway 4 run (Karlis kick)
NY —Safety; Elway tackled in end
      zone by Martin
NY —Bavaro 13 pass from Simms
      (Allegre kick)
NY —FG Allegre 21
NY —Morris 1 run (Allegre kick)
NY —McConkey 6 pass from Simms
      (Allegre kick)
Den—FG Karlis 28
NY —Anderson 2 run (kick failed)
Den—V. Johnson 47 pass from Elway
      (Karlis kick)

SUPER BOWL XX

CHICAGO vs. NEW ENGLAND

What happens when the NFL's best rushing team meets the league's best defense? That was the question of sports fans nationwide in the days before Super Bowl XX. The game would pit the powerful running game of the New England Patriots against the tough defensive unit of the Chicago Bears.

The New England Patriots featured running backs Craig James and Tony Collins slashing for big yardage behind the league's top-rated offensive line. James and Collins were a potent one-two punch in the New England backfield. James ran for 1,227 yards and a 4.7 average during the 1985 regular season. Collins added another 657 rushing yards. He also led the team with 52 pass receptions coming out of the backfield.

Center Pete Brock anchored the Patriots' fine offensive line. He was flanked by guards John Hannah and Ron Wooten and tackles

Steve Moore and Brian Holloway. Tight end Lin Dawson rounded out this spectacular group. The running game helped the Pats to an 11-5 record, earning a wild card spot in the play-offs.

But history was against the Patriots. The 19 previous Super Bowl games featured only one team that went from a wild card start to a Super Bowl victory. The Pats, however, put away their history books and played tough football. They whipped the New York Jets 26-14, then upset the Los Angeles Raiders 27-20. The Pats earned the Super Bowl berth by pounding Miami 31-14 for the AFC championship. In the three play-off wins, New England averaged 49 rushing plays and only 14 passing plays.

But they were to meet a defensive unit that was already being called the best in the long history of the NFL. The Chicago Bears' defense didn't just beat its 1985 opponents. It beat them up! And when the defenders had thoroughly pounded the opposing offense, Jim McMahon and Walter Payton and the other offensive Bears came in to score some big points.

The Bears on defense were led by linebackers Mike Singletary and Wilber Marshall. On the defensive front were Dan Hampton, Steve McMichael, and Richard Dent, along with rookie star William "the Refrigerator" Perry. Gary Fencik and Dave Duerson headed up the secondary. Five of the eleven were bound for the Pro Bowl—the NFL all-star game—after the Super Bowl.

This defense led the Bears to a 15-1 record during the 1985 regular season. The Miami Dolphins ruined the perfect mark in the season's thirteenth week. In the play-offs, the Bears blasted the New York Giants 21-0 and the Los Angeles Rams 24-0 in the play-offs. It was the first time in NFL history that any team had shut out both of its play-off opponents. In the process, Chicago shut down running stars Joe Morris of the Giants and Eric Dickerson of the Rams.

The Bears were one of the oldest, most famous franchises in the NFL. They had been the powerhouse in the early years of the league in the 1920s, 30s, and 40s. But they had fallen on hard times since and hadn't won a championship since 1963—before anyone had ever heard the words *Super Bowl!*

The Superdome in New Orleans was filled with 73,818 rowdy fans. They didn't have to wait very long for some excitement. On the second play of Super Bowl XX, Chicago running back Walter Payton fumbled. New England linebacker Larry McGrew recovered the loose ball at the Bears' 19-yard line.

The Patriots surprised the football world during its first possession. This running team came out passing the football! Quarterback Tony Eason's first pass fell incomplete. His second pass went in and out of the hands of wide receiver Stanley Morgan. The third pass was wild, with Eason under major pressure from blitzing Chicago linebackers.

So the Patriots had to settle for a Tony Franklin field goal. The Pats took a 3-0 lead over the favored Bears with only 1:19 gone in the game. It was the earliest score in Super Bowl history.

Chicago drove back to tie the game on its next possession. The Bears started the drive at their 31-yard line. After a first down, quarterback Jim McMahon hit sprinter Willie Gault with a pass. Gault turned the play into a 43-yard gain. He was finally dropped at the New England 10-yard line. Four plays later, Kevin Butler kicked a 28-yard field goal to tie the game at 3-3.

New England's offense returned to the field after the kickoff. Surely, everyone thought, the Pats would go back to what got them to the Super Bowl—running the football. But head coach Raymond Berry still had passing on his mind. But Tony Eason couldn't find the mark. He fired two straight incompletions. On third down he dropped back to pass once again. Defensive end Richard Dent and linebacker Wilber Marshall stormed into the pocket and sacked Eason. The Patriots had yet to try a running play.

"They tried to lull us to sleep by saying they were going to run, run, run," said Chicago defensive tackle Steve McMichael later. "Then they come out throwing."

"I wanted to establish the fact that we had to throw the ball," answered Berry after the game. "I didn't think we could just run the ball and cram it down the Bears' throats."

When the Patriots got the ball back, they did finally try a running play. Craig James was stopped for no gain. Then Eason went back to pass. He was crushed by defensive linemen Richard Dent and Steve McMichael. The football popped loose. Defensive end Dan Hampton recovered the fumble at the New England 13-yard line. But the Patriot defense held the Bears on downs. Kevin Butler's field goal gave Chicago a 6-3 lead.

Disaster struck the Pats again on their next possession. Craig James took a handoff and started to sweep around the left side. Dent stood up the running back and stripped away the football. Mike Singletary jumped on the fumble at the New England 13-yard line. Bear quarterback Jim McMahon faked a handoff to superstar Walter Payton and gave the ball

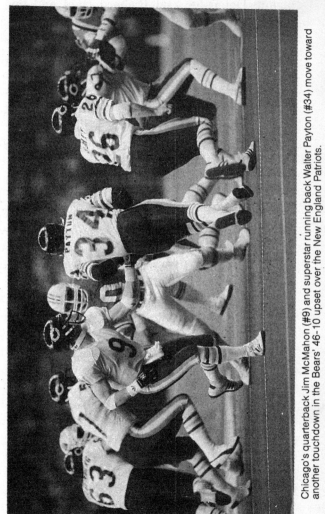

Chicago's quarterback Jim McMahon (#9) and superstar running back Walter Payton (#34) move toward another touchdown in the Bears' 46-10 upset over the New England Patriots.

Focus West Photo

to fullback Matt Suhey, who gained 2 yards. McMahon again faked to Payton and gave to Suhey. This time Suhey popped free for an 11-yard touchdown run. Butler booted the extra point. Chicago took a 13-3 lead with only 23 seconds left in the first quarter. The Patriots ran one more play in the opening period. Craig James ran for three yards. It was the only New England play in the first quarter that gained any yardage.

Eason and the New England offense failed to move the ball in the second quarter. But Chicago quarterback Jim McMahon had no problem. Early in the period, he launched a 10-play, 59-yard drive that resulted in another score. A big 24-yard pass from McMahon to Matt Suhey was the key play in the drive. McMahon himself scored the TD on a 2-yard scamper. Butler's kick gave the Bears a 20-3 lead halfway through the period.

The next New England possession ended in another crushing sack of quarterback Tony Eason. This time it was blitzing linebacker Otis Wilson who crunched the QB. Tony Eason was finished for the day. He had completed none of his six passes and had been sacked three times. Coach Berry replaced Eason with veteran Steve Grogan late in the first half.

The half ended with another Chicago surge.

McMahon passed to wideouts Dennis Gentry and Ken Margerum in moving his offense down the field. The 11-play, 72-yard drive ended with a Kevin Butler field goal of 25 yards as the clock ran down. Chicago led 23-3 at halftime.

The nasty Chicago defense had enjoyed a spectacular first half. The Bears held New England to a record-setting minus 19 yards in the first half!

The Bears came out roaring in the second half. They ended New England's first possession when Otis Wilson sacked quarterback Steve Grogan. They began their own first possession with a 60-yard bomb from Jim McMahon to speedy Willie Gault. This led to a killer 96-yard drive that ate up the clock. It also dashed any dim hopes for victory the Patriots may have still held. The drive wrapped up with McMahon's second short TD run of the game. Kevin Butler kicked his third PAT. The score was 30-3.

Just a minute later, rookie defensive back Reggie Phillips intercepted a Steve Grogan pass. Phillips legged out a 28-yard touchdown. Butler kicked another extra point. Chicago's lead was now 37-3. Turn out the lights!

A few minutes later, Craig James lost another fumble. Chicago's Wilber Marshall recovered, pitched to Otis Wilson, and the ball ended up at New England's 37-yard line. Five plays later, the Fridge, 308-pound defensive tackle William Perry, carried 1 yard for another TD. Butler's kick made it 44-3.

Late in the third period, the Patriots finally moved into plus yardage for the game. Grogan directed the Patriots on a 15-play, 76-yard drive. His passes started connecting. He hit wide receivers Stephen Starring and Stanley Morgan with big throws. Early in the fourth quarter, the Pats finally scored a touchdown. Grogan hit wide receiver Irving Fryar with an 8-yard TD toss. Tony Franklin kicked the PAT. The score was still an out-of-sight 44-10. But New England had at least scored a touchdown. That was something no other team had managed in the 1985 play-offs against Chicago.

Chicago defensive leader Buddy Ryan pulled all but one of his starters for the last 9:43 of the game. At that point, the Bears had allowed only 81 total yards to New England's offense. The Patriots got 42 yards the rest of the way for 123 total. That came within four yards of the lowest total in Super Bowl history. Had Chicago's starters stayed in for the entire game, the record would certainly have been theirs.

It seemed only right the Bears' defense accounted for the final points of Super

Bowl XX. Back-up defensive tackle Henry Waechter sacked Grogan in the end zone with 5:36 left in the game. The safety gave the Bears their final 46-10 margin of victory.

The final statistics tell the incredible story of the Bears' total defensive domination. The Pats gained only seven rushing yards on 11 plays for an average of 0.6 yards per carry. Tony Collins was the leading ground-gainer with a measly four yards on three carries. Back-up QB Grogan did complete 17 of 30 passes for 177 yards. But seven sacks of Grogan and starter Tony Eason erased 61 of those passing yards.

Defensive end Richard Dent was named the MVP. Dent was superhuman early in the game. He forced two fumbles, earned one-and-a-half sacks, and pressured the Pats' quarterbacks on nearly every passing play.

Chicago's offense played well, too. Quarterback Jim McMahon completed 12 of 20 passes for 256 yards. He ran for two touchdowns. Superstar running back Walter "Sweetness" Payton gained 61 yards in 22 carries while acting as decoy much of the game. As a result, running mate Matt Suhey ran for 52 key yards in just 11 carries. The Bears' offense ran up 408 total yards. The 46 points scored by the Bears set a Super Bowl record. So did the 36-point margin of victory.

36-point margin of victory.

"There's no question that we're the better football team," said Chicago head coach Mike Ditka in the loud championship locker room. "You can analyze it any way you want and we're still the better team." Ditka should know about championship football. He played tight end on the the Bears' 1963 title team.

"We're the best defense of all time," added Bear safety Dave Duerson. "No question. Look at the total yards. That'll tell you. The Super Bowl is supposed to be the best two teams in the National Football League, and we totally dominated them. We knew if we executed it would be a blowout."

Jim McMahon, the brash and wild quarterback for the Bears, became a celebrity by the end of Super Bowl XX. He constantly changed headbands on the sidelines and mugged for the television cameras. And perhaps he best summed up the Super Bowl experience for fans of the mighty Bears.

"It was fun out there!" said the grinning quarterback.

Chicago	13	10	21	2	—	46
N. Eng.	3	0	0	7	—	0

NE—FG Franklin 36
Chi—FG Butler 28
Chi—FG Butler 24
Chi—Suhey 11 run (Bulter kick)
Chi—McMahon 2 run (Butler kick)
Chi—FG Butler 25
Chi—McMahon 1 run (Butler kick)
Chi—Phillips 28 interception return
  (Butler kick)
Chi—Perry 1 run (Butler kick)
NE—Fryar 8 pass from Grogan
  (Franklin kick)
Chi—Safety; Grogan tackled in end zone
  by Waechter

SUPER BOWL
XIX

MIAMI vs. SAN FRANCISCO

The year 1984 was a record-breaking kind
of season in the NFL. Eric Dickerson, a
brilliant young runner for the Los Angeles
Rams, broke O.J. Simpson's "unbreakable"
single-season rushing record. And the Chicago
Bears' veteran runner Walter Payton broke
Jim Brown's "unbreakable" career rushing
record.

In any normal NFL season, Dickerson and
Payton would have been the talk of the league.
But 1984 was no normal NFL season. It was
the year of "Dangerous Dan" Marino of the
Miami Dolphins.

Dickerson and Payton were great. Marino
was incredible. The second-year quarterback
shattered two of the NFL's oldest records. He
became the first NFL quarterback ever to
throw for more than 5,000 yards in a season.
And he tossed a record-exploding 48 touchdown passes. In an *average* game, Marino

threw for 320 yards and three touchdowns. That's a career high for many quarterbacks! For Marino, that was just another Sunday at the ball park.

Dangerous Dan led his Dolphins to a 14-2 regular season record. The Dolphins ran away with the AFC East title. They scored the most points in the NFL. They cruised through the play-offs. They ripped Seattle 31-10 behind four Marino TD passes. They crushed Pittsburgh 45-28 behind Marino's three scoring tosses. As the Dolphins prepared for Super Bowl XIX, the eyes of the football world were on Dan Marino.

But the 49ers had a pretty decent QB of their own, a guy named Joe Montana. Their 15-1 record was the best in the NFL. The 49ers handily won the NFC West title. Their defense was the toughest in the NFL. San Francisco opened the play-offs with a 21-10 romp over the Giants. Then the 49ers crushed Chicago 23-0 in the NFC title game. A win in the Super Bowl would be the 49ers' eighteenth victory of the season. No NFL team had ever before won more than 17 games in a season.

A crowd of 84,059 in Stanford Stadium near Palo Alto, California saw Marino and the Dolphins get off to a big start, with two scoring drives in the first quarter. The Dolphins' first possession began on their own 36. Marino stepped back to pass and fired out to running back Tony Nathan in the flat. Nathan juked, spun and raced downfield for a 25-yard gain. It looked like Marino and the Dolphins were in for a big day. The drive ended in a 37-yard field goal by Uwe von Schamann, giving Miami a 3-0 lead.

San Francisco quickly struck back. Montana keyed the 49ers' first TD drive by running and passing. On third-and-seven from Miami's 48, Montana dropped back to pass. Miami defensive end Kim Bokamper barrelled in for the sack. Montana slipped Bokamper's tackle and raced 15 yards down the sideline for a big first down. On the next play, Montana rolled to the right. Running back Carl Monroe slipped out of the backfield. Montana hit Monroe with a perfect pass. The speedy running back eluded safety Lyle Blackwood's tackle and raced into the end zone. The 33-yard TD and Ray Wersching's extra point gave San Francisco a 7-3 lead.

Miami coach Don Shula knew the 49ers liked to make a lot of defensive substitutions after every play. So Shula ordered Marino to work without a huddle. After every play, the Dolphins raced to the line of scrimmage for another snap. This gave San Francisco no time for changes.

The plan worked. Marino hit tight end Dan

Johnson with a 21-yard pass. He fired to wide receiver Mark Clayton for 13 yards. He hit wide receiver Mark "Super" Duper with an 11-yard completion. The drive ended with a 2-yard touchdown pass from Marino to Johnson. Von Schamann's extra point gave Miami a 10-7 lead.

The first quarter ended at 10-7. The 17 points set a Super Bowl record for the first quarter. Marino completed 9 of 10 passes in the period. "Dangerous Dan" was having a field day.

Joe Montana's scrambling hurt Miami once again as the second quarter got going. He scrambled for 19 yards. Montana then passed to wide receiver Dwight Clark for a 16-yard gain. From the Dolphins' 8-yard line, Montana hit running back Roger Craig with a touchdown pass for a 14-10 lead early in the second quarter.

After a short Reggie Roby punt gave San Francisco the ball at its own 45, it then took Montana only six plays to produce another TD. Suddenly, the 49ers had a 21-10 lead. Nearly half the second quarter remained.

Marino started to have his problems against San Francisco's highly rated defense. The no-huddle offense no longer worked. The 49ers had adjusted by using an unusual 4-1-6 defense. Four linemen rushed Marino. One

San Francisco 49ers' Roger Craig flies across the goal line for a touchdown against Miami.

linebacker played short pass defense or blitzed the quarterback. Six defensive backs covered Miami's speedy receivers. This kind of defense dared Marino to throw. He kept throwing. He kept coming up empty. And when the Dolphins tried running, San Francisco's defensive line blasted the ball carriers after short gains.

Another short Reggie Roby punt set up another 'Niner touchdown. This drive started at the 49ers' 48-yard line. Nine plays and 52 yards later, Roger Craig blasted over from the 3-yard line. It was 28-10, 'Niners!

Miami did manage to move the ball on its next possession. Marino hit some short passes and a 30-yarder to tight end Joe Rose. The drive ended in a 31-yard von Schamann field goal with 12 seconds left in the first half. The kick cut San Francisco's lead to 28-13.

On the next kickoff, von Schamann bounced a short kick to the 49ers. Then guard Guy McIntyre smothered the ball. The half should have ended there. But McIntyre got up and started to run. He was smashed by Miami's Joe Carter. The football popped loose, and Miami's Jim Jensen recovered the shocking fumble. Von Schamann kicked a 30-yard field goal with four seconds left in the half.

The first half ended with San Francisco ahead 28-16. The 49ers' 28 points and the combined 44 points were new Super Bowl records for scoring in a half

The Dolphins had ideas of a comeback in the second half. But the San Francisco defense began to dominate the game. The 4-1-6 defense completely shut down Miami's running attack. Marino was forced to pass on play after play. Miami's offensive line was forced into strength-draining pass blocking on play after play.

Soon the weary linemen started giving ground to San Francisco's brutal pass rush. Marino found himself surrounded by red and gold uniforms on every pass play. He rushed his passes. He tried to scramble. He threw too long. He threw too short.

The sacks began in the second half. Dwaine Board got to Marino twice. Manu Tuiasosopo and Gary "Big Hands" Johnson each sacked Marino once. Four sacks against Miami was big news. The Dolphins had allowed only 14 sacks in the 18 games up to Super Bowl XIX.

And with the sacks came the interceptions. Eric Wright made an acrobatic interception to save a touchdown pass in the third quarter. Carlton Williamson stole a misguided Marino aerial in the end zone in the fourth quarter. For the first time in his pro career, Marino threw more interceptions (two) than TD passes (one) in a game.

San Francisco scored a field goal in the third quarter to end a 10-play, 43-yard drive. A Montana 12-yard scramble was the key play in the drive. Wersching kicked a 27-yarder to give San Francisco a 31-16 lead. Montana put together a final drive late in the third quarter, starting at his own 30. Montana passed 30 yards to Wendell Tyler and 13 yards to Russ Francis. The drive ended with Joe Montana's third TD pass of the game, 16 yards to Roger Craig.

Super Bowl XIX finished as a blowout, 38-16. The margin of victory was the second widest in Super Bowl history. The 49ers' 38 points tied the Super Bowl record for most points.

Joe Montana was named MVP. He completed 24 of 35 passes for a Super Bowl record of 331 yards and three touchdowns. He also ran five times for 59 important yards and a touchdown.

San Francisco's offensive and defensive units shared the credit for the lopsided victory. The offense amassed a Super Bowl record 537 total yards. The defense allowed the fewest rushing yards in Super Bowl history (25). Marino also set two Super Bowl records. His 50 passes and 29 completions were both records.

"Joe Montana had his greatest game of the

year," said 49er head coach Bill Walsh. "And the fact that we put the pressure on Marino made a lot of difference."

As Walsh clutched the Vince Lombardi trophy in the victorious locker room, he praised his team. He called the 49ers "the greatest team playing football today."

Nobody was about to disagree!

Miami	10	6	0	0	—	16
San Francisco	7	21	10	0	—	38

Miami—FG von Schamann 37
SF   —Monroe 33 pass from Montana
        (Wersching kick)
Miami—Johnson 2 pass from Marino
        (von Schamann kick)
SF   —Craig 8 pass from Montana
        (Wersching kick)
SF   —Montana 6 run (Wersching kick)
SF   —Craig 3 run (Wersching kick)
Miami—FG von Schamann 31
Miami—FG von Schamann 30
SF   —FG Wersching 27
SF   —Craig 16 pass from Montana
        (Wersching kick)

SUPER BOWL XVIII

WASHINGTON vs. LOS ANGELES RAIDERS

Somewhere along the line, Marcus Allen got a bum rap. People said he wasn't fast enough. They said he'd never be a game-breaker. It all started during Allen's senior year at the University of Southern California. USC had been the home of great running backs, from Mike Garrett and O.J. Simpson to Charles White.

Allen rushed for an incredible 2,342 yards in 1981, his senior season. He won the Heisman Trophy, awarded to the best player in college football. But when the 1982 NFL draft came around, Marcus Allen was passed over. The word was out. The 6-foot-1, 210-pound Allen was too slow to star in the NFL. Sixteen teams passed over Allen in the 1982 draft. Finally, the Los Angeles Raiders drafted him. Allen was a typical Raider selection. The Raiders had a reputation for choosing guys who were either too small, too slow, or too old to cut it with other teams.

In 1983, Allen proved the Raiders were right.

He ran for 1,014 yards and 9 touchdowns. He helped the Raiders, recently moved from Oakland, to a 12-4 regular season record. The Raiders won the AFC West title. Allen really turned it on in the play-offs. He gained 121 yards in a 38-10 slaughter of the Pittsburgh Steelers. Then, in the AFC title game, he busted for 154 yards against the Seattle Seahawks. L.A. won the game 30-14.

The Raiders headed for Super Bowl XVIII. But the Washington Redskins were ready for them. The Redskins had won Super Bowl XVII and had roared through a 14-2 regular season, with both losses by a single point. The Redskins crushed the Los Angeles Rams by 51-7 to open the play-offs. Then they edged an excellent San Francisco team 24-21 in the NFC title game.

Only three teams had ever won back-to-back Super Bowls, the Green Bay Packers, the Pittsburgh Steelers (twice) and the Miami Dolphins. The Redskins wanted to be the fourth team to win back-to-back Super Bowls. They also wanted to be the first team since 1972 (and the second team ever) to win 17 games in a single NFL season. A crowd of 72,920 jammed into Tampa Stadium for that Florida city's first-ever Super Bowl. At kickoff, the Redskins were favored by three points.

The first break went to the Raiders. The Redskins failed to move the ball on their first

Raiders' Marcus Allen, #32, beats out the Washington Redskins for a 74-yard touchdown.

possession. Jeff Hayes set up to punt on fourth down from the Redskins' 30-yard line. The snap from center Jeff Bostic was high, but Hayes pulled it down. As a result, Hayes was a half-step slow in getting off the punt. By then, Raider special teams captain Derrick Jensen had smashed up the middle. He blocked the punt. The ball headed toward the goal line. There was a huge pileup in the end zone. At the bottom of the pile, cradling the football, was Derrick Jensen. Touchdown, Raiders! Chris Bahr's kick gave Los Angeles a 7-0 lead only five minutes into the game.

The Redskins recovered an L.A. fumble on the next series. But the drive stalled and Mark Moseley missed a 44-yard field goal attempt. The Raiders had the wind to their backs in the second quarter. Quarterback Jim Plunkett started airing out the football. Plunkett lobbed a bomb to speedster wide receiver Cliff Branch for a 50-yard gain. Two plays later Plunkett found Branch alone in the end zone. The 13-yard TD pass and Bahr's kick gave L.A. a 14-0 lead. Less than six minutes remained in the first half.

Washington responded with its first long drive of the half. Quarterback Joe Theismann, throwing against the wind, hit three of five passes in marching the 'Skins down the field. The key play was an 18-yard completion to Alvin Garrett. But the drive ran out of gas at the Los Angeles 7-yard line. Moseley chipped a 24-yard field goal. With three minutes left in the first half, the Raiders led 14-3.

The 'Skins got the ball back at their own 12-yard line with 12 seconds left in the half. Most teams would have run out the clock since being behind at halftime was no big deal in the NFL.

But the Redskins set up for a pass play. When Theismann dropped back to pass, it looked like a long bomb was in the works. Theismann looked deep. Then he whirled and looked to the left flat. A screen play was forming for Redskin running back Joe Washington. Theismann lobbed the pass over the outstretched hands of defensive end Lyle Alzado.

But, from out of nowhere, a black jersey streaked past Washington. Linebacker Jack Squirek intercepted the soft pass and danced into the end zone. Squirek was mobbed by his teammates. The Raiders had a 21-3 lead at halftime.

The Redskins needed a big comeback in the second half. The third quarter started well for the Redskins. Theismann marched the 'Skins on a 70-yard TD drive. Fullback John Riggins scored the touchdown on a 1-yard run. The TD put Riggins in the record books. He became the first player in NFL history to score a touchdown in six straight play-off games. Moseley's extra point try was blocked by tight end Don Hasselback. The Redskins trailed 21-9 with 11 minutes left for third quarter. They were still in the game.

The Raiders rose to Washington's challenge. Plunkett led an eight-play, 70-yard drive that ended in a Marcus Allen touchdown run of 5 yards. L.A.'s lead was 28-9 halfway through the third quarter.

Late in the quarter, Washington recovered a fumble at the Los Angeles 35-yard line. A touchdown would put the Redskins back into the game. After three plays, the ball rested on the 26-yard line, fourth-and-one. Washington coach Joe Gibbs kept the offense on the field. Theismann handed off to big John Riggins. A swarm of black jerseys converged on Riggins. When they cleared away the pileup, Riggins was short of the first down. The ball went over to Los Angeles. There was time for one more play in the third quarter.

And what a play it turned out to be! Plunkett took the snap and handed off to Allen. Led by a pulling guard, Allen started a sweep to the left side. Redskin defenders closed in. So Allen whirled around and started back to the right. He slipped a tackle behind the line of scrimmage. A wall of black-jerseyed blockers set up in front of him. Suddenly he was in the clear. Allen galloped untouched for a 74-yard touchdown. The man called "too slow" had just made the longest TD run in the history of the Super Bowl and the NFL play-offs. The Raiders led 35-9.

Allen provided most of the excitement in the

fourth quarter. He broke loose for a 39-yard gain late in the game to set up a Bahr field goal, giving the Raiders a 38-9 lead.

That's how it ended. Marcus Allen carried the ball 20 times for a Super Bowl record 191 yards and scored two touchdowns. His bum rap days were over for good. He was named Most Valuable Player of Super Bowl XVIII.

Raider quarterback Jim Plunkett, MVP in Super Bowl XV, had another fine outing in the rout of the Redskins. He completed 16 of 25 passes for 172 yards and a touchdown. The Raiders now owned three Super Bowl trophies. Only the Pittsburgh Steelers, with four, had won more.

Wash.	0	3	6	0	—	9
L.A.	7	14	14	3	—	38

LA —Jensen recovered blocked punt in end zone (Bahr kick)

LA —Branch 12 pass from Plunkett (Bahr kick)

Wash—FG Moseley 24

LA —Squirek 5 interception return (Bahr kick)

Wash—Riggins 1 run (kick blocked)

LA —Allen 5 run (Bahr kick)

LA —Allen 74 run (Bahr kick)

LA —FG Bahr 21

SUPER BOWL XVII

MIAMI vs. WASHINGTON

John Riggins has always marched to the beat of a different drummer.

There was the time he let his hair grow so long and bushy that his helmet couldn't fit over his head.

And there was the time he shaved his head, except for a Mohawk running down the middle.

Then there was the time he retired because he was bored with football.

And there was the time he fell sound asleep at a party. But this wasn't just any old party. The vice president of the United States was there. And Riggins was seated at a table with a Supreme Court justice. Riggins, clad in a tuxedo, snored loudly during the vice president's speech.

The 6-foot-2, 235-pound Riggins began his career with the New York Jets. He had a couple of good seasons with New York. But he came alive after a trade to Washington. His 1,014 yards were fifth highest in the NFC in 1978. His 1,153 yards were sixth highest in the NFC in 1979. He also finished third in the NFC in touchdowns that year.

Riggins retired in 1980 and the Redskins slumped from 10-6 in 1979 to 6-10 in 1980. Big John "un-retired" and returned in top form in 1981. He gained 714 rushing yards and scored 13 touchdowns. The Redskins rebounded to 8-8.

Riggins became a quiet, determined player in 1982. He refused to talk to the media. He concentrated on football. He rushed for 553 yards in the nine games of the strike-shortened season. His bullish running took the pressure off Joe Theismann and the 'Skins' passing attack. Theismann led the NFC in passing. The defense rallied behind the reborn offensive attack. Washington allowed the fewest points in the NFL (128) and finished with the league's best record (8-1).

Big John went crazy in the play-offs. He reeled off three straight 100-yard rushing games. He helped the Redskins to victories over Detroit (31-7), Minnesota (21-7), and Dallas (31-17). Riggins' 444 yards in three play-off games gave the Redskins an 11-1 record and a berth in Super Bowl XVII.

The Miami Dolphins rode a solid defense

and a big-play offense into a 7-2 regular season in 1982. Young quarterback David Woodley was starting for the first time. Second-year running back Andra Franklin provided most of the ground game. The "Killer Bees" defense—named because the last names of many of the starters began with the letter *B*—dominated the AFC all season long. The Dolphins led the league in pass defense and finished second to the Redskins in scoring defense. The Killer Bees shut down quarterback Steve Grogan and the New England Patriots 28-13. Then Miami's defense crushed Dan Fouts and the San Diego Chargers 34-13. In the AFC title game, the Dolphins whitewashed Richard Todd and the New York Jets, 14-0. They were favored by three points in Super Bowl XVII in California's Rose Bowl.

After a slow start and an exchange of punts, Miami had the ball on its own 24-yard line. It was second-and-six. Woodley took the snap and rolled to his right. He pumped once, then fired a soft pass into the flat. Wide receiver Jimmy Cefalo caught the ball in the space between cornerback Jeris White and safety Tony Peters. Cefalo faked White and headed down the sideline. Peters missed the tackle. Cefalo, suddenly all alone, cut back into the center of the field and raced for the end zone. None of the Redskins came close to catching him. Uwe von Schamann's kick gave Miami a 7-0 lead with seven minutes gone in the first quarter.

But Woodley went from hero to goat when he coughed up the football after a hard hit by defensive end Dexter Manley. Nose tackle Dave Butz recovered the ball at Miami's 46-yard line. From there the Redskins went into a conservative rushing offense. Theismann handed off to Big John Riggins again and again. Riggins bulled for four and five yards a carry. The drive stalled at Miami's 14-yard line. Riggins carried on five of the eight plays in the drive. Mark Moseley kicked a 31-yard field goal to cut Miami's lead to 7-3.

Fulton Walker of Miami juked and jived his way to 42-yard return of the next kickoff. The return inspired a Miami drive. Woodley ran the offense through a time-consuming 13-play, 50-yard drive. But Miami lost steam at Washington's 3-yard line. Uwe von Schamann kicked a 20-yard FG to give Miami a 10-3 lead with six minutes to go in the first half.

The Redskins put together their best drive of the first half on their next possession. Washington started at its own 20-yard line. Theismann, at the order of coach Joe Gibbs, stuck with the ground game. Seven of the next ten plays were runs, mostly by Riggins. The runs opened up the passing attack.

Washington's John Riggins, #44, escapes tackle from Miami's Don McNeal, #28. Riggins was named the game's Most Valuable Player.

Theismann hit tight end Rick Walker for 27 yards. Then he hooked up on a screen pass with Riggins for 15 more yards. A 12-yard scramble by Joe Theismann moved the ball to Miami's 13. On the first play after the two-minute warning, Theismann hit wide receiver Alvin Garrett with a 4-yard touchdown pass. The 11-play, 80-yard drive and Moseley's kick tied up the game at 10-10.

The tie didn't last very long. Fulton Walker caught Moseley's kickoff at the 2-yard line. He started to the right. Then he cut back to the left. The speedy Dolphin suddenly broke into the open. He raced 98 yards for a touchdown, the longest kickoff return in Super Bowl history!

"My first reaction when it was over was to look for a flag," admitted Walker afterward. There were no flags. Miami led 17-10 with 1:38 left in the half.

The Redskins didn't just run out the clock after that. Theismann led the Washington offense in a perfect drive down the field. Perfect, that is, until the very end. With 14 seconds left in the half, and no time-outs remaining, Theismann hit Alvin Garrett with a pass at Miami's 7-yard line. Garrett struggled to get out of bounds to stop the clock. The Dolphins tackled him, and he didn't make it. The clock ticked down.

Washington's field goal team was still setting up when the half ended. The Redskins lost out on an almost sure field goal. The half ended with Miami ahead 17-10.

"I knew I made a stupid play," admitted Joe Theismann later.

Washington's defense got tough in the third quarter. In fact, the 'Skins so completely shut down Woodley that he didn't complete another pass in the entire game. And while the defense was dominant, Washington's offense slowly built momentum of its own.

A trick play led to the only score of the third quarter. Theismann took the snap at his own 47-yard line. He faked the handoff. Then he pitched back to wide receiver Alvin Garrett on the reverse. Garrett sped around the end and into the open. Then he raced all the way to Miami's 9-yard line before being tackled.

"It was wide open," said Garrett. "All I had to do was take the ball and run. It was the perfect time to call it, and it was perfectly executed."

But Miami's Killer Bees didn't give up. They stopped Washington at the 3-yard line. Moseley's field goal cut Miami's lead to a shaky 17-13.

The rest of the third quarter was scoreless. Both teams failed to take advantage of opportunities. Miami linebacker A.J. Duhe intercepted a Theismann pass in Washington territory. But Woodley turned around and threw an interception of his own. Mark Murphy made a diving interception of Woodley's tipped bomb at Washington's 4-yard line.

One play near the end of the third quarter summed up Miami's futility. Theismann dropped back to pass from deep in his own territory. Miami defensive end Bokamper slammed in and blocked Joe Theismann's pass. The ball floated straight into the air. Bokamper waited for the catch and easy touchdown. But somehow, Theismann got in and knocked the ball down.

Miami carried its 17-13 lead into the fourth quarter. The Dolphins fought off the Redskins' next attack. Lyle Blackwood intercepted a Theismann pass at Miami's 1-yard line. But Miami's offense once again failed to move the ball and Washington took over at its own 48-yard line. And this time there was no stopping Big John Riggins.

The Redskins faced fourth-and-one at Miami's 43-yard line. Then Gibbs signaled Theismann to go for it. The Redskins lined up with just over 10 minutes left in Super Bowl XVII. Theismann barked out the signals. Everyone knew what was coming. Theismann took the snap and handed off to Riggins.

Miami's Killer Bees were wedged in tightly on the short-yardage play. Riggins exploded through the left side of the line. He shed a last-ditch tackle attempt by defensive back Don McNeal. Big John Riggins swept down the field, over the goal line, and into the record books.

The Redskins mobbed the giant fullback. With 10:01 left in Super Bowl XVII, Washington led for the first time. Mark Moseley's kick gave the 'Skins a 20-17 lead. Riggins' TD run was the longest in Super Bowl history up to that time. And it gave the Redskins an edge that they would never let go. The defense forced Miami to run three plays and then punt. The Redskins got the ball back at Miami's 41-yard line. The clock read 8:42 left to play in the game.

Riggins dominated the rest of the game. The Redskins chewed up the clock and chewed up Miami's proud Killer Bees. With 1:55 left in the game, Theismann passed 6 yards to Charlie Brown for the insurance TD. The touchdown ended a 12-play, 6:47 drive. Mark Moseley's kick gave the 'Skins a 27-17 advantage.

Miami's coach Don Shula brought in veteran quarterback Don Strock to rally the Dolphins. But it was too late. Strock fired three incomplete passes and the Redskins claimed their first Super Bowl victory 27-17.

MVP Riggins finished with 166 yards rushing on 38 carries. The loneliest Dolphin in the lonely locker room was defensive back Don McNeal. He was the only Dolphin with even the slightest chance of stopping Riggins' TD run for glory. "I was there," admitted McNeal. "I had the position, but he's very physical, a tough guy to bring down."

Riggins' 166 rushing yards nearly edged Miami's entire offensive output for the day. The Dolphins managed only 176 total yards against the inspired Washington defense. And 76 of those yards came on the single TD pass play. The Redskins' defense held Woodley to 4 of 14 passing, including 0-for-8 in the second half. Washington's Theismann hit on 15 of 23 passes for 143 yards and a pair of touchdowns. The 'Skins totaled 400 offensive yards against the respected Killer Bees of Miami.

Miami	7	10	0	0	— 17
Wash.	0	10	3	14	— 27

Miami—Cefalo 76 pass from Woodley
        (von Schamann kick)
Wash —FG Moseley 31
Miami—FG von Schamann 20

Wash —Garrett 4 pass from Theismann
      (Moseley kick)
Miami—Walker 98 kickoff return
      (von Schamann kick)
Wash —FG Moseley 20
Wash —Riggins 43 run (Moseley kick)
Wash —Brown 6 pass from Theismann
      (Moseley kick)

SUPER BOWL XVI

CINCINNATI vs. SAN FRANCISCO

There was a new look to Super Bowl XVI. It would be the first Super Bowl to be played in a cold weather location—the Pontiac Silverdome, near Detroit. The match-up was another first. The San Francisco 49ers and the Cincinnati Bengals broke a string of 12 straight Super Bowls played by at least one repeater. First-timers hadn't met in a Super Bowl since Super Bowl III, when the Jets and Colts were both newcomers.

And this game saw the first appearance of a player who many people think is the greatest ever to play in the Super Bowl.

In 1981 the Bengals and 49ers surprised everyone by roaring through the regular season and into Super Bowl XVI. Cincinnati posted a 12-4 record. The Bengals edged Buffalo, 28-21, in the first round of the play-offs. Then they crushed San Diego, 27-7, in below-zero weather to win the AFC title.

The 49ers won 12 of their last 13 games en route to a 13-3 record, the best in the NFL. They beat the New York Giants in the first round of the play-offs and edged the Cowboys 28-27 in the NFC championship game.

The 49ers won the coin toss and decided to receive. But San Francisco didn't have the ball for very long. Amos Lawrence suffered from super-jitters and fumbled the ball. Cincinnati's John Simmons recovered the ball at San Francisco's 26-yard line. The Bengals had a huge break to start Super Bowl XVI.

A quick pass from Bengal QB Anderson to Isaac Curtis moved the ball down to the 18. Then a pass to tight end Dan Ross moved Cincy down to the 8. It looked as if the Bengals would draw first blood. But San Francisco's defense said no way. The 49ers stopped Charles Alexander for no gain. Defensive end Jim Stuckey threw Anderson for a sack back to the 11. On third down Anderson made a very big mistake. He threw his pass right into the arms of 49ers safety Dwight Hicks. Hicks returned the interception 27 yards to his own 32.

The Bengals had wasted their first chance. The 49ers were determined not to waste theirs. Quarterback Joe Montana started moving his offense down the field. A screen pass netted six yards. A short flare pass got six more. A Montana toss to wide receiver Freddie Solomon picked up nine yards. It was third-and-one.

Most teams would have run their fullback up the middle. But not the 49ers. Joe Montana handed off to running back Ricky Patton. Patton handed off to wide receiver Freddie Solomon. Solomon faked a reverse and then pitched back to Montana. The strong-armed QB then hit tight end Charlie Young on a big first down pass.

Then the fired-up 49ers drove right in for the score. Fullback Earl Cooper busted for 10 yards. Running back Bill Ring popped for six. Montana hit Young with a pass. Young was dropped at the 1-yard line. Montana sneaked across for the first touchdown of Super Bowl XVI. Ray Wersching's kick gave the 49ers a 7-0 lead.

Cincinnati got rolling early in the second period. Anderson hit rookie receiver Cris Collinsworth with an 18-yard pass down to San Fran's 28. A couple of plays later Anderson hit Collinsworth again. Collinsworth was blasted at the 5-yard line by defensive back Eric Wright, and the ball popped loose. 'Niner cornerback Lynn Thomas came up with it at the 8. The Bengals had once more thrown away a chance to score.

Joe Montana again took advantage of the

break. He directed his offense on an incredible 12-play, 92-yard scoring drive. Montana mixed up runs by his backs with short passes. The 49ers slowly ate up the field. Montana hit Young for a 20-yard gain. Montana passed to Dwight Clark for 11 more. A late hit penalty moved the ball down to Cincinnati's 10-yard line.

From the 10, Montana sent fullback Earl Cooper on a delay pattern in the left flat. Somehow Cooper was wide open. Montana lofted a soft pass to the big back. Cooper grabbed the pass and rumbled into the end zone. Wersching's kick gave the 49ers a 14-0 lead with seven minutes left in the half. The 92-yard drive was the longest in Super Bowl history. Fans began to wonder if maybe there wasn't something definitely special about this Montana guy.

The Bengals failed to move on their next possession. The 49ers started moving again from their own 34-yard line. Montana hit Clark for a quick 17 yards. Patton knocked off 10 yards on back-to-back carries. Short passes to Cooper and Clark put the ball down at the Cincinnati 20-yard line. Less than a minute was left in the half. Montana and Young hooked up on a pass play down to the 5. From there, Wersching kicked a 22-yard field goal. With just 15 seconds left in the half, San

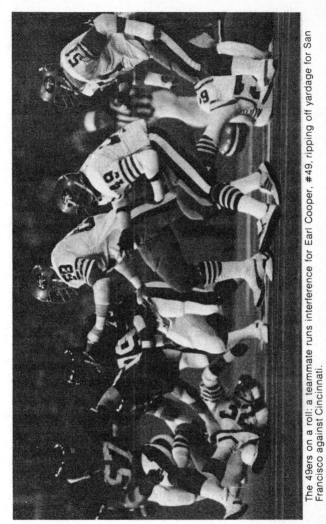

The 49ers on a roll: a teammate runs interference for Earl Cooper, #49, ripping off yardage for San Francisco against Cincinnati.

Francisco had a 17-0 lead.

But the 49ers weren't finished yet. Ray Wersching squibbed his kickoff across the artificial turf. Bengal after Bengal tried to grab the madly bouncing ball. San Francisco's Milt McCall finally pounced on the fumble at the Cincinnati 5-yard line. Wersching kicked a 27-yard field goal, and the 49ers had a 20-0 halftime lead—the largest in Super Bowl history. The odds were definitely stacked against the Bengals.

But the Bengals quickly proved they weren't out of it. Ken Anderson directed an impressive 83-yard scoring drive to start the second half. Then Pete Johnson and Charles Alexander did most of the ground work. Anderson hit wide receiver Steve Kreider on a big 19-yard play. A razzle-dazzle pitch and pass to Isaac Curtis moved Cincy down to the 49er 23-yard line. A roughness penalty moved the ball to the 11. Three plays later Ken Anderson scrambled five yards up the middle for a TD. Jim Breech booted the extra point. San Francisco's lead was cut to 20-7.

Cincinnati's defense came alive, too. Twice the Bengals forced the 49ers to punt. Cincy's offense got the ball back at midfield late in the third period. Once again Anderson drove the Bengal offense right down the field. The biggest offensive play in the drive was a 49-

yard Anderson bomb to Collinsworth. The rookie receiver was dragged down at the San Francisco 15-yard line. Four plays later, the Bengals had a first down at the 49er 3-yard line.

What followed was an awesome goal-line stand by the San Francisco defense. Pete Johnson, the 250-pound Bengal fullback, bulled to the 1 on first down. On second down Johnson was hammered back to the 2 by linebacker Jack "Hacksaw" Reynolds. On third down Anderson tossed a little flare pass to Charles Alexander. Alexander caught the pass, but linebacker Danny Bunz caught Alexander and wrestled him down at the 1-yard line.

Fourth and 1. *Everything* rode on the next play. Anderson handed off to Johnson. Johnson crashed into the line. There he was met by Hacksaw Reynolds, Bunz, Ronnie Lott and Archie Reese. Johnson never even got close to the goal line. The 49er defenders did a victory dance off the field.

The goal-line stand killed a Bengal drive. But Cincy was far from finished. The clock clicked into the fourth quarter. Cincinnati was down 20-7.

Anderson engineered another scoring drive early in the final period. He hit Collinsworth for 11. He hit tight end Dan Ross for 10. A pass interference penalty put the ball on the San Francisco 15. Anderson hit Ross again for 10. The final Anderson-Ross connection resulted in a 5-yard TD. Breech kicked the extra point. Cincinnati had closed the gap to 20-14 with 10:06 left in the game.

But Montana and the 49er offense responded to the Bengal challenge. Montana hit Mike Wilson for a big 23-yard gain. Ricky Patton rambled for several short gains. A sneak by Montana, a run by Cooper and two short gainers by Patton set up a field goal try. Wersching was good on the 40-yard kick. With only 5:25 left, the 49ers had some breathing room—with the score 23-14.

Cincinnati's comeback try ended when defensive back Eric Wright intercepted an Anderson pass at the Bengal 48-yard line and returned it to the 22. A smiling Wright cradled the football and ran off the field. He had just become the first rookie to intercept a pass in the Super Bowl. Six plays later Wersching made his fourth field goal. San Francisco had a 26-14 lead with 1:57 remaining in the game.

But the Bengals still refused to quit. Ken Anderson went to work from his own 26. He hit Isaac Curtis for 21 yards. He hit Ross for 15 and again for 8. He hit Collinsworth for 9. He hooked up with Kreider for 17 yards. From the 49er 3-yard line, Anderson passed to Ross for the touchdown. Breech's kick was good. The score was 26-21.

But there were only 16 seconds left.

The Bengals tried an onside kick. Dwight Clark recovered the ball for San Francisco. The 49ers lined up for a final play. Montana took the snap and fell to the ground. There he was mobbed by teammates as the clock ticked down to zero. After 36 long years, the 49ers owned their first NFL championship. The 49ers carried coach Bill Walsh off the field.

Montana completed 14 of 22 passes for 157 yards with one touchdown and no interceptions to win his first MVP award. San Francisco's only turnover was the fumble on the game's opening kickoff. The Bengals, on the other hand, turned the ball over four times. Two interceptions marred Ken Anderson's fine performance. He completed 25 of 34 passes for 300 yards and had two touchdowns.

San Francisco   7   13   0   6 —   26
Cincinnati   0   0   7 14 —   21
SF—Montana 1 run (Wersching kick)
SF—Cooper 11 pass from Montana
        (Wersching kick)
SF—FG Wersching 22

SF —FG Wersching 26
Cin—Anderson 5 run (Breech kick)
Cin—Ross 4 pass from Anderson
     (Breech kick)
SF —FG Wersching 40
SF —FG Wersching 23
Cin—Ross 3 pass from Anderson
     (Breech kick)

SUPER BOWL XV

OAKLAND vs. PHILADELPHIA

Super Bowl XV in New Orleans will always be remembered as the game between the good guys and the bad guys. But the bad guys, who were also owned by the bad guy, had a good guy as their leader!

The Oakland Raiders were considered the bad guys by football fans. The Raiders had a lot of players who had been traded away by other teams for discipline problems. Even Raiders owner Al Davis was considered an outlaw. He threatened all year to move his team to Los Angeles. The other NFL owners wanted the Raiders to stay put. Al Davis was not the most popular guy in pro football circles.

But Raider QB Jim Plunkett, a great college star who had never really become a star in the NFL, had worked hard to become a starter. For his performance, he was named NFL Comeback Player of the Year.

Oakland's Jim Plunkett attempts a first down but is stopped by Philadelphia.

The Raiders surprised everyone by making it to Super Bowl XV, only the second wild card team to make it. But their opponents, the Philadelphia Eagles, had knocked on the door in 1978 and 1979. In 1980 they were ready for their first shot at the big game. The Eagles were the good guys. Coach Dick Vermeil had the toughest training camp and strictest rules of any NFL coach.

The bad-guy Raiders struck first. Plunkett tossed a TD pass to speedy wideout Cliff Branch after Raider linebacker Rod Martin had picked off Eagle QB Ron Jaworski's pass. Oakland led 7-0.

The Eagles came roaring right back. Jaworski fired a long one to wide receiver Rodney Parker. Parker made a grab in the end zone, and the Eagles began celebrating.

But their joy didn't last long. A yellow flag rested on the turf. The touchdown was called back because of an illegal procedure penalty. Instead of a TD and a tied score, the Eagles had to punt.

Oakland took quick advantage of the Philly flub. A scrambling Plunkett floated a pass to running back Kenny King at his own 35-yard line. He turned upfield, and when it was over, King had an 80-yard touchdown play! And the Raiders had a 14-0 lead. Philly got a Tony Franklin FG and the score at halftime stood at 14-3, Oakland.

The third quarter saw more Raider offensive fireworks. Plunkett hit Branch for another touchdown, stretching the Raiders' lead to 21-3. It was off to the races when linebacker Martin picked off his second Jaworski pass, and Oakland got another Chris Bahr field goal. The bad guys led 24-3.

The Eagles finally scored a touchdown early in the fourth quarter. An 88-yard drive ended with a scoring pass from Jaworksi to tight end Keith Krepfle. With 14 minutes remaining, Philly closed the gap to 24-10.

But Oakland answered the Eagle TD with a long offensive drive that ended with another field goal. Oakland upped its lead to 27-10. Then Rod Martin pounded the final nail in the Philly coffin with his Super Bowl-record third interception. The Raiders became the first wild card team to win a Super Bowl.

And Jim Plunkett, the good guy who had almost retired in frustration at the beginning of the season, completed 13 of 21 passes for 261 yards and three touchdowns. He was named MVP of Super Bowl XV.

| Oakland | 14 | 0 | 10 | 3 | — | 27 |
| Philadelphia | 0 | 3 | 0 | 7 | — | 10 |

Oak—Branch 2 pass from Plunkett (Bahr kick)
Oak—King 80 pass from Plunkett (Bahr kick)
Phil—FG Franklin 30
Oak—Branch 29 pass from Plunkett
    (Bahr kick)
Oak—FG Bahr 46
Phil—Krepfle 8 pass from Jaworski
    (Franklin kick)
Oak—FG Bahr 35

SUPER BOWL XIV

PITTSBURGH vs.
LOS ANGELES RAMS

Super Bowl XIV matched a team everyone thought would make it to the big one, the defending champ Steelers, with a team no one thought would make it, the Los Angeles Rams. The Rams brought the worst record in Super Bowl history to the game, 11-7. Over 100,000 fans packed the Rose Bowl in Pasadena, California to see how the hometown Rams would do against the three-time champion Steelers.

No one was surprised when the Steelers drove right down the field on their first possession. But the Ram defense held and forced the Steelers to settle for a Matt Bahr field goal. The Steelers led 3-0.

But after the Rams took the kickoff, QB Vince Ferragamo and his offensive teammates marched right down the field. They took a 7-3 lead when big fullback Cullen Bryant blasted into the end zone from a yard out.

Pittsburgh's Franco Harris plows through the Rams' defensive line on his way to a first down.

Then a good nine-play drive by signal-caller Terry Bradshaw and the Steelers had the lead again. Running back Franco Harris got the last yard. It was now 10-7, Steelers.

The game seesawed back and forth. L.A. tied the game on a Frank Corral FG. Then they got another chance after an interception. Corral connected on a 45-yarder with just 24 seconds left in the half. The heavy underdog Rams took a 13-10 lead into the locker room at halftime!

The Steelers knew they were in a battle when they took the field for the second half. Had they underestimated the Rams? Was a tremendous upset in the cards?

Coach Chuck Noll and his Pittsburgh coaching staff decided to open up the offense in the third quarter. Right away, Bradshaw fired a long pass to wide receiver Lynn Swann. Ram defenders had Swann well covered. But Swann leaped high into the air and made one of his famous incredible catches for a TD, giving the Steelers a 17-13 lead.

The Rams showed some of their long ball offense during the next big drive. Ferragamo tossed a 50-yard bomb to Ram's wide receiver Billy Waddy. The Rams scored on a trick play, a halfback pass from Lawrence McCutcheon to Ron Smith. L.A. led, 19-17. Was the Steeler reign over?

But the Steelers had some offensive fireworks left. Early in the fourth quarter, Terry Bradshaw dropped back to pass from his own 27. He connected with another Steeler super wide receiver, John Stallworth, on a 73-yard TD bomb. 24-19, Pittsburgh. The lead had changed hands six times!

But the Rams weren't finished yet. With just five minutes remaining, Ferragamo drove his troops to the Pittsburgh 32. He faded back to pass. He fired deep for the winning score. But Steeler Hall-of-Fame linebacker Jack Lambert cut in front of the Ram receiver and picked off the pass. Then Bradshaw broke the Rams' heart with a long, clock-eating drive that included a long bomb to Stallworth. When Franco Harris finally plowed into the end zone from the Ram 1-yard line, it was all over. The underdog Rams had put up a great fight, but the Steelers were now four-time Super Bowl champs. And for the second year in a row, Terry Bradshaw was named Super Bowl MVP.

Los Angeles   7   6   6   0 — 19
Pittsburgh   3   7   7 14 — 31

Pitt—FG Bahr 41
LA —Bryant 1 run (Corral kick)

Pitt—Harris 1 run (Bahr kick)

LA —FG Corral 31

LA —FG Corral 45

Pitt—Swann 47 pass from Bradshaw
  (Bahr kick)

LA —Smith 24 pass from McCutcheon
  (kick failed)

Pitt—Stallworth 73 pass from Bradshaw
  (Bahr kick)

Pitt—Harris 1 run (Bahr kick)

PITTSBURGH vs. DALLAS

Super Bowl XIII in the Orange Bowl was the first rematch in the game's history. The Steelers had beaten the Cowboys 21-17 in Super Bowl X. Both teams had won two Super Bowl trophies. And both teams wanted to be the first ever to win three.

Everyone expected Super Bowl XIII to be exciting. Pittsburgh's Terry Bradshaw had thrown the most touchdown passes (28) in all of pro ball in 1978. Dallas' Roger Staubach had been rated the number-one quarterback in the league.

Then the first break in the game went in Pittsburgh's favor. Pittsburgh's Banaszak recovered a fumbled Dallas handoff at the Steeler 34-yard line. Bradshaw found acrobatic wide receiver John Stallworth in the end zone. A twisting, leaping catch gave the Steelers the early lead, 7-0.

The Cowboys tied the game late in the first

125

quarter, when Bradshaw was smacked by Dallas defensive end Harvey Martin. Defensive end Ed "Too Tall" Jones recovered at the Pittsburgh 41-yard line. Two plays later, wide receiver Tony Hill took a short pass from Staubach and turned it into a 39-yard touchdown scamper. The first quarter ended 7-7.

The Dallas defense made things happen again in the second quarter. Linebacker Mike Hegman stripped the ball out of Bradshaw's hands as he tried to pass and raced 37 yards with the stolen ball for an easy touchdown. Dallas was up 14-7.

But the Steelers tied it up seconds later. Bradshaw dropped back to pass from his own 25-yard line. He hit Stallworth again with a short pass. But Stallworth turned upfield, broke a few tackles, and was gone! His 75-yard touchdown run knotted the score at 14 all. But just before halftime, after a Mel Blount interception, Bradshaw found RB Rocky Bleier in the endzone. Pittsburgh had a 21-14 lead at halftime.

The game may have been decided in the third period. From the Pittsburgh 10-yard line, Staubach faked the run up the middle. Veteran tight end Jackie Smith was wide open in the end zone for a sure TD. Staubach lofted a soft pass. Smith slipped, fell, and the ball bounced off his hands. The Cowboys had to settle for a 27-yard field goal by Rafael Septien. That made the score 21-17.

Then the Steelers really went to work. A Franco Harris run and a Lynn Swann reception after a Dallas fumble gave Pittsburgh two TDs for a 35-17 lead. But the Cowboys weren't dead yet. Staubach drove the explosive Dallas offense right down the field, hitting tight end Billy Joe DuPree for a 7-yard touchdown pass. Pittsburgh's lead was cut to 35-24.

And when Dallas recovered an onside kick at its own 47-yard line, Staubach set his sights on the end zone once again. With 22 seconds left in the game, he tossed a touchdown strike to wide receiver Butch Johnson. The Cowboys were down 35-31.

The Cowboys tried another onside kick. But there were no more miracles and Rocky Bleier of the Steelers recovered. Seconds later it was over. The Steelers had become the first team ever to win three Super Bowls.

Football fans everywhere were already calling it the greatest of all Super Bowl games. Bradshaw had completed 17 of 30 passes. Stallworth caught three for 115 yards and two touchdowns. Swann caught seven for 124 yards and one touchdown. The Steelers put on the greatest passing show in Super Bowl history that day. For his record-setting performance, Terry Bradshaw was named

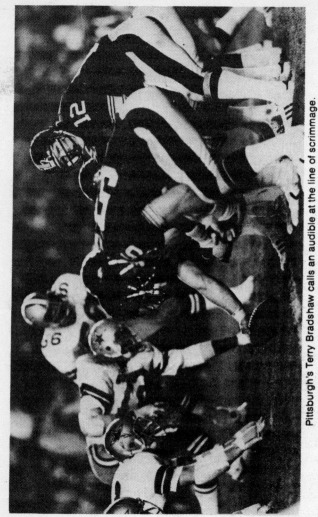

Pittsburgh's Terry Bradshaw calls an audible at the line of scrimmage.

Most Valuable Player.

"We knew Bradshaw was the key, and we didn't stop him the way we had to," said Dallas safety Cliff Harris. "They are really a good team, but Bradshaw made them great today. He deserved the MVP."

```
Pittsburgh   7  14   0  14  —  35
Dallas       7   7   3  14  —  31
```

Pitt—Stallworth 28 pass from Bradshaw
    (Gerela kick)
Dal—Hill 39 pass from Staubach
    (Septien kick)
Dal—Hegman 37 fumble recovery
    (Septien kick)
Pitt—Stallworth 75 pass from Bradshaw
    (Gerela kick)
Pitt—Bleier 7 pass from Bradshaw
    (Gerela kick)
Dal—FG Septien 27
Pitt—Harris 22 run (Gerela kick)
Pitt—Swann 19 pass from Bradshaw
    (Gerela kick)
Dal—Dupree 7 pass from Staubach
    (Septien kick)
Dal—Johnson 4 pass from Staubach
    (Septien kick)

DENVER vs. DALLAS

Before the start of Super Bowl XII in New Orleans, former teammates Craig Morton and Roger Staubach met at the middle of the field. Morton was in the uniform of the Denver Broncos. Staubach wore the colors of the Dallas Cowboys. Morton and Staubach had played together for the Cowboys for almost six seasons. They were about to battle it out for the football championship of the world. Only one of the veteran quarterbacks would end the day a champion.

Super Bowl XII matched Denver's Orange Crush defense against Dallas' Doomsday II defense. Everyone expected a super Super Bowl game. A super mistake by the Cowboys in the first few minutes of the game almost gave Denver an early edge. Dallas punt return ace Tony Hill took a Denver punt near his own end zone. He fumbled the kick and there was a scramble for the ball. The

Dallas' defensive end Randy White hits the arm of Denver's quarterback Craig Morton. Morton's pass was intercepted by Dallas' Randy Hughes.

UPI Photo

Cowboys were lucky. Aaron Kyle recovered the ball at his own 1-yard line.

As it turned out, the Cowboys got the first break when Dallas defender Randy Hughes intercepted Morton's pass at the Denver 25-yard line. Running back Tony Dorsett took the ball in and Dallas led 7-0. When Denver got the ball again, disaster struck again! This time, the pass was tipped by linebacker Bob Breunig and intercepted by Aaron Kyle. Dallas had the ball at the Denver 35-yard line. Two Cowboy field goals made the lead 13-0.

Denver's problems continued for the rest of the first half. The Doomsday II defense held the Denver offense. It didn't help that the Broncos lost three fumbles and had four Morton passes picked off! Morton had thrown only eight interceptions all season long. But the Orange Crush defense kept the game close. Even though Denver lost the ball seven times on turnovers, Dallas had managed only 13 points. The Broncos were still in it!

Kicker Jim Turner got the Broncos on the board in the third quarter with a 47-yard field goal. The Dallas lead was cut to 13-3. But the Cowboys answered with a drive of their own late in the third quarter. Staubach hit wide receiver Butch Johnson on a long bomb. Johnson made a leaping, diving catch in the end zone for a 20-3 Dallas lead.

But the Broncos didn't give up. Rick Upchurch received the kickoff following the touchdown at his own 7. He scrambled left, wiggled right, and streaked up the field. He was finally stopped at the Dallas 26-yard line. But when the Denver offense took the field, it was without Craig Morton. Coach Red Miller had decided to go with a younger, faster quarterback.

Norris Weese came in and took only four plays to lead Denver to a touchdown. Denver had closed the gap to 20-10. And there was still plenty of time left. But yet another fumble gave Dallas the ball at the Broncos' 29. Then Dallas delivered the knockout punch.

Staubach gave the ball to running back Robert Newhouse. He pretended he was running a sweep play. Suddenly, Newhouse stopped and threw a perfect TD pass to Golden Richards! The Dallas lead was 27-10 and Denver was down and out.

It was the second Super Bowl victory for Dallas against two losses. It was also the first Super Bowl win for the NFC after five straight AFC victories.

Dallas' Doomsday II defense had a special reason to celebrate. Defensive tackle Harvey Martin and defensive end Randy White had just been named the Most Valuable Players in Super Bowl XII, the only time two players shared the honor.

Dallas	10	3	7	7	—	27
Denver	0	0	10	0	—	10

Dal— Dorsett 3 Run (Herrera kick)

Dal— FG Herrera 35

Dal— FG Herrera 43

Den—FG Turner 47

Dal— Johnson 45 pass from Staubach (Herrera kick)

Den—Lytle 1 Run (Turner kick)

Dal— Richards 29 pass from Newhouse (Herrera kick)

SUPER BOWL XI

OAKLAND vs. MINNESOTA

Fran Tarkenton had just about done it all in his 16 years of pro football. He was considered one of the best quarterbacks ever to play the game. He had broken passing records held by some of the biggest names in NFL history. He had led his Minnesota Vikings to several conference titles.

But there was one prize that Fran hadn't claimed—a Super Bowl ring. The Vikings played in three of the first nine Super Bowl games. Tarkenton was the quarterback in two of those games. The Vikings lost every time. Now they had another chance. Their opponents—the Oakland Raiders, coached by John Madden. The Raiders were also looking for their first Super Bowl victory. Oakland had lost to the Green Bay Packers way back in Super Bowl II.

Over 100,000 people gathered in the Rose Bowl in Pasadena. They saw Tarkenton's

Vikings get the first big break in the game. Late in the first period, the Raiders were in punt formation deep in their own territory. Minnesota linebacker Fred McNeill burst through the line and blocked Ray Guy's punt! It was the first Ray Guy punt that had ever been blocked by anyone. McNeill fell on the football at the Oakland 3-yard line. Things were looking good for the Vikes. But when Fran Tarkenton handed off to running back Brent McClanahan, the football popped out. Oakland linebacker Willie Hall recovered.

Quarterback Kenny (The Snake) Stabler brought the Oakland offense to life after the recovery. Stabler directed a long drive down to the Minnesota 7-yard line. From there, Errol Mann kicked a field goal to give the Raiders a 3-0 lead. The Snake led the Raiders to another FG and a TD that half. He relied on the running of Clarence Davis and his own pinpoint passing to tight end Dave Casper and wide receiver Fred Biletnikoff. The Raiders had a 16-0 lead at halftime.

Tarkenton and the Vikes had played another disappointing first half of a Super Bowl game. In all four games the Vikings had failed to score in the first half. The AFC opponents had a 51-0 total halftime lead on the Vikings in the four Super Bowls!

But even though the Vikings came out for

the second half more determined than ever, Oakland scored first. Another Errol Mann FG upped the Raider lead to 19-0.

Tarkenton finally got his offense moving late in the third period. He hit rookie wide receiver Sammy White for a touchdown, cutting the Oakland lead to 19-7. But another Minnesota drive was ended by a Willie Hall interception.

Then Snake Stabler went for the kill. A long pass to Biletnikoff and a few running plays, and suddenly it was 26-7. Tarkenton was forced to pass on every play to catch up. He made the mistake of throwing at 14-year pro veteran defensive back Willie Brown. Brown made the Vikings pay. He picked off the pass at his own 25-yard line and returned it 75 yards for a spectacular touchdown. Oakland had a 32-7 lead, and time was running out— again—for the Vikes.

Time had run out for Fran Tarkenton. Coach Bud Grant replaced him with Bob Lee. Tarkenton sat on the bench for the final minutes of his last Super Bowl. Lee moved the Vikings for a final TD, but it didn't make any difference. The game ended Oakland 32, Minnesota 14.

The Vikings had lost their fourth Super Bowl against no victories. The Raiders had won their first after an earlier loss. Fred

Oakland's Fred Biletnikoff catches a Ken Stabler pass at the Minnesota one yard line.

UPI Photo

Biletnikoff won MVP honors for his spectacular catches. Clarence Davis was another offensive star for the Raiders. He picked up 137 yards in just 16 rushing attempts.

It was another day of super frustration for Fran Tarkenton and the Minnesota Vikings.

```
Oakland     0  16  3  13  —  32
Minnesota   0   0  7   7  —  14
```

Oak —FG Mann 24
Oak —Casper 1 pass from Stabler
      (Mann kick)
Oak —Banaszak 1 run (kick failed)
Oak —FG Mann 40
Minn—S. White 8 pass from Tarkenton
      (Cox kick)
Oak —Banaszak 2 run (Mann kick)
Oak —Brown 75 interception return
      (kick failed)
Minn—Voigt 13 pass from Lee (Cox kick)

SUPER BOWL X

PITTSBURGH vs. DALLAS

By the time Super Bowl X rolled around, a lot of fans were grumbling that the game was always boring, that there were no exciting, big plays. But Super Bowl X brought together a pair of teams who liked to score points—the defending champion Pittsburgh Steelers and the first wild card team to make it to the Super Bowl, the Dallas Cowboys. Even though both had excellent defenses, each also had a dynamite offense.

"I don't know how it's going to turn out," said Pittsburgh Coach Chuck Noll of the game in the Orange Bowl. "I think it might come down to the big play." Fans hoped that Noll was right. And he was!

Cowboy QB Roger Staubach went right to work after Pittsburgh punter Bobby Walden fumbled. Roger the Dodger fired a perfect TD toss to wide receiver Drew Pearson. Dallas had the early lead, 7-0.

Pittsburgh wasted no time in coming back. Running backs Franco Harris and Rocky Bleier moved the ball to the Dallas 48-yard line. Then Terry Bradshaw fired a pass down the sideline. Lynn Swann made an incredible catch before going down at the Dallas 15-yard line. Three plays later, a TD pass to tight end Randy Grossman tied the score.

The Steelers had several chances to score during the second quarter, but they came away with nothing. Gerela missed on two field goal tries, wasting another unbelievable diving, juggling catch of 53 yards by Lynn Swann. The Cowboys took a 10-7 lead into the locker room on a Toni Fritsch field goal.

The defenses controlled the third quarter, and the score was still Dallas 10, Pittsburgh was 7 at the start of the fourth period. Then the Steelers got a big break when Reggie Harrison blocked Mitch Hoopes' punt out of the Cowboy end zone for a safety. It was now 10-9, Dallas.

Soon after, Roy Gerela kicked a 36-yard field goal to give the Steelers the lead for the first time, 12-10. Pittsburgh got another big play minutes later. Mike Wagner intercepted a Roger Staubach pass and returned the ball to the Cowboys' 7-yard line. But again the Dallas defense held. Gerela's field goal gave the Steelers a 15-10 lead.

Dallas couldn't move on its next possession and the Steelers took over. Bradshaw faked a handoff and faded back to throw the bomb. And there was Lynn Swann again, running under the ball. Touchdown, Pittsburgh! The play covered 64 yards—another big play by Swann. With 3:22 left, Pittsburgh had a 21-10 lead.

But the Cowboys weren't dead. In only 34 seconds, Roger Staubach found Percy Howard for a 34-yard touchdown pass. It was Howard's first and only catch as a pro player. It was now 21-17, Steelers, with 2:48 left in the game!

The Dallas defense forced Pittsburgh to punt and Staubach brought his offense onto the field with 1:22 left in the game. Fans had seen plenty of miracle finishes from Staubach. Could he do it again?

It looked that way. Staubach drove the Cowboys to the Pittsburgh 37. But then Pittsburgh's Glen Edwards picked off a pass to end the Dallas threat and preserve the Steelers' second straight Super Bowl victory. Roger had run out of miracles. Edwards ran off the field waving the ball in the air. "We're number one!" screamed Pittsburgh fans.

No one was surprised when Lynn Swann was named the Most Valuable Player. He caught

Pittsburgh's Lynn Swann dives for a 53-yard gain.

UPI Photo

four passes for 161 yards. And every catch
was spectacular!


```
Dallas       7  3  0  7  — 17
Pittsburgh   7  0  0 14  — 21
```

Dal —D. Pearson 29 pass from Staubach
    (Fritsch kick)
Pitt—Grossman 7 pass from Bradshaw
    (Gerela kick)
Dal —FG Fritsch 36
Pitt—Safety, Harrison blocked punt
    through end zone
Pitt—FG Gerela 36
Pitt—FG Gerela 18
Pitt—Swann 64 pass from Bradshaw
    (kick failed)
Dal —Howard 34 pass from Staubach
    (Fritsch kick)

SUPER BOWL IX

PITTSBURGH vs. MINNESOTA

"Give me a D!" screamed the fans of the Pittsburgh Steelers.

"Give me a D!" shouted the fans of the Minnesota Vikings.

For fans of both teams, "D" stood for only one thing—defense! Tulane Stadium in New Orleans was filled with 80,997 football fans, every one of them expecting Super Bowl IX to be a magnificent defensive battle.

The Steelers were making their first appearance in the big one. They were led by their tough-as-nails defense, the Steel Curtain. Minnesota's defense had a nickname, too—the Purple People-Eaters. The Vikes had lost their first two Super Bowl games. And they wanted this one in a big way.

As expected, neither offense could move the ball. The first quarter ended in a 0-0 tie. The Steelers were the first in the game to score, early in the second quarter. But it wasn't the Pittsburgh offense that did the scoring.

Minnesota had the ball at its own 10-yard line. Quarterback Fran Tarkenton faked a pitch-out and then tried to hand off to running back Chuck Foreman. But the ball bounced off Foreman's hip. The ball rolled into the end zone. Tarkenton finally fell on it. And then a Steeler fell on Tarkenton! The safety gave the Steelers a 2-0 lead.

There was another wild play in the first half. Tarkenton threw a pass. It was blocked by Pittsburgh defender L.C. Greenwood. The ball dropped right back into Tarkenton's hands. So he threw another pass—and completed it to John Gilliam! But the officials called the play back. It was illegal to throw two forward passes on the same play.

A Steeler interception at the goal line stopped a Viking drive at the end of the half. The half ended with a baseball-like score of 2-0 in favor of Pittsburgh. But it wasn't the Pittsburgh Pirates over the Minnesota Twins! So far, the fans were right. The defensive teams were running the show.

The second half began with another strange play. Pittsburgh kicker Roy Gerela slipped and fell as he kicked off. The ball bounced down the field. Minnesota's Bill Brown grabbed it, but he couldn't hold on to it. Pittsburgh's Marv Kellum recovered the fumble at the Minnesota 30-yard line.

The Steelers were finally able to capitalize on the break. With big running back Franco Harris doing most of the work, the Steelers scored the first touchdown of Super Bowl IX, for 9-0 lead.

The Vikings got their biggest break of the day early in the fourth quarter. A pass interference call on Pittsburgh's Mike Wagner gave the Vikings a first down at the Pittsburgh 5-yard line. A touchdown would pull the Vikings to within two points. There was still plenty of time left.

But again the powerful Steel Curtain did the job. Steeler tackle Mean Joe Greene forced a fumble by the Vikings' Chuck Foreman. Mean Joe recovered it, killing yet another Viking drive.

But the Vikings weren't out of it yet! The Purple People-Eaters kept the Steelers from moving after Joe Greene's fumble recovery. Minnesota's Matt Blair raced through the line and blocked Bobby Walden's punt. Terry Brown grabbed the ball in the end zone for a Minnesota touchdown. The extra point kick by Fred Cox hit the goal post and bounced away. But the Vikings had narrowed Pittsburgh's lead to 9-6 with over 10 minutes left. The tension in the air was something else!

The Steelers started on offense from their

Pittsburgh's Franco Harris looks for an open hole after receiving the ball from quarterback Terry Bradshaw.

own 34-yard line. Steelers' quarterback Terry Bradshaw handed off to Franco Harris. He handed off to Rocky Bleier. He handed off to Harris again. And again. The Steelers drove down the field, using up the clock. Harris and Bleier both ran for first down after first down.

Then, with the ball on the Minnesota 4-yard line, Bradshaw faked another running play. And then he tossed a short pass to tight end Larry Brown. Touchdown, Pittsburgh! The score was 16-6 with 3:31 left in the game. The Pittsburgh offense moved 66 yards and used nearly seven minutes of the clock.

The Vikings got the ball back. But they were shut down again by the Steel Curtain. The Steelers won their first title, 16-6, after 42 years in the league. For the Vikings it was their third loss in three Super Bowl games. The Pittsburgh defense had held the Vikings to a tiny 17 yards on 21 rushing attempts. The Minnesota offense scored no points. Running back Franco Harris earned MVP honors. He carried 34 times for 158 yards, breaking Larry Csonka's 1974 record.

The Steelers had looked so tough that day that fans had a feeling they might see more of the team in black and gold in future Super Bowls. And they were right!

```
Pittsburgh   0   2   7   7  — 16
Minnesota    0   0   0   6  —  6
```

Pitt —Safety, Tarkenton tackled in end zone
Pitt —Harris 9 run (Gerela kick)
Minn—Brown, fumble recovery in end
      zone (kick failed)
Pitt —L. Brown 4 pass from Bradshaw
      (Gerela kick)

MIAMI vs. MINNESOTA

Only one team had ever won back-to-back Super Bowls—the Green Bay Packers. But in Super Bowl VIII another team was trying to join the legendary Pack as double winners. The Miami Dolphins had won Super Bowl VII. A triumph in Super Bowl VIII over the Vikings would match the Packers.

The fans who gathered in Houston's Rice Stadium expected a battle between famous quarterbacks and tough defenses. Miami's Bob Griese and Minnesota's Fran Tarkenton were two of the best quarterbacks in the NFL. And Miami's "No-Name Defense" joined Minnesota's "Purple People-Eaters" as the toughest in the league.

The Dolphins took the opening kickoff. And they quickly made it clear that their game plan was ball-control all the way! Bruising fullback Larry Csonka—the Zonk—crashed up the middle for good yardage on almost every carry. It took the Dolphins 10 plays to move 62 yards. Csonka scored on a 5-yard run, and Miami led 7-0. The Vikings hadn't even touched the ball.

The Miami "D" proved just as tough as its ball-control offense, and the Vikes had to punt. The Dolphins went straight back up the field once again with Zonk doing most of the damage. At the end of the first quarter it was 14-0, Miami. The Dolphins had run 20 offensive plays. The Vikings had run 3. Could Tarkenton and the Vikings come back?

Minnesota was able to mount a solid drive late in the second quarter. But it died on the Dolphin 6-yard line when running back Oscar Reed fumbled the ball away. The half ended with the Dolphins on top 17-0. They had made it look easy. Griese had to throw only six passes the entire half, and completed five.

Minnesota opened the second half with a big play. John Gilliam received the Miami kickoff and took off on his return. Gilliam returned the kickoff 65 yards to the Miami 34-yard line. But a penalty brought the exciting play back. Minnesota had to start at its own 11-yard line instead of the Miami 34-yard line. The Vikings failed to move the ball. Miami's offense took over once more.

The second half was more crunching running from Csonka and Kiick, with some passes

Miami's quarterback Bob Griese watches the action after completing a pass to Paul Warfield.

mixed in. Receiver Paul Warfield made a stupendous catch that led to a Miami TD. The No-Name defense also held the Vikes in check until the end of the game. Tarkenton ran for the first—and only—score of the afternoon for Minnesota. Super Bowl VIII ended Miami 24, Minnesota 7.

The MVP was no surprise. It went to Zonk, for the most awesome display of power running yet seen in a Super Bowl. He carried the ball 33 times for 145 yards, both Super Bowl records. He scored two touchdowns.

And Miami joined Green Bay as the only teams to win two Super Bowls in a row. Some people later said that they had never seen *any* team play as well as the Dolphins did that day in Houston. They called those 1973 Miami Dolphins one of the greatest NFL teams of all time. And none of the Minnesota Vikings were about to disagree!

Miami   14 3 7 0 — 24
Minnesota   0 0 0 7 —   7

Miami—Csonka 5 run (Yepremian kick)
Miami—Kiick 1 run (Yepremian kick)
Miami—FG Yepremian 28
Miami—Csonka 2 run (Yepremian kick)
Minn —Tarkenton 4 run (Cox kick)

MIAMI vs. WASHINGTON

Sixteen victories and no defeats. That's the record the Miami Dolphins took into the Super Bowl VII in Los Angeles. No pro football team had ever gone through the regular season undefeated. But they still had to prove they were the best by winning the Super Bowl.

The Washington Redskins were the team the Dolphins had to beat to go 17-0. The 'Skins were no pushovers. In the NFC title game, they had smashed the defending champ Cowboys 26-3.

The Dolphins and Redskins were very different teams. The Dolphins were young, but cool and calm. Washington was a veteran team that played emotional football. Miami's defense was nicknamed the "No-Name Defense." The Redskins were called the "Over-the-Hill Gang."

Miami quarterback Bob Griese was young. He threw a picture-perfect spiral pass.

Miami's safety Jake Scott intercepts a pass thrown by Washington's Billy Kilmer.

UPI Photo

Washington quarterback Billy Kilmer had played pro ball for a long time. His passes were called "wounded ducks" because they wobbled their way to receivers. But both quarterbacks were winners.

Defense controlled the early part of the game. Neither team could do much against the other's "D." But Griese finally got the Miami running game moving late in the first quarter. Running backs Larry Csonka, Jim Kiick and Eugene "Mercury" Morris all popped for short gainers. Then Griese hit wide receiver Howard Twilley on a 28-yard TD strike! It was 7-0, Dolphins.

An interception by Miami linebacker Nick Buoniconti late in the half gave the Dolphins the ball at the Washington 27-yard line. Griese went right to work. Tight end Jim Mandich made a diving catch at the 2-yard line. Two plays later Jim Kiick bulldozed in for the score. Miami led 14-0 at the half.

The defenses were awesome in the second half. Washington's only real threat ended in a missed field goal. Both teams stalled. Time was running out on the Redskins when Dolphin kicker Garo Yepremian came out to try a 42-yard boot.

What followed was one of the most famous disasters in Super Bowl history. Yepremian kicked the ball. The Redskins blocked it. The ball bounced back to Garo. He picked it up. He ran with it. He held it up to try to pass to a teammate. But the ball slipped out of his hand. In the confusion, Washington's Mike Bass picked the ball out of the air and went all the way for a 49-yard touchdown!

Suddenly it was 14-7. And there was enough time left for the Redskins to pull the great upset. Washington got the ball back with 74 seconds left—one last chance. But the No-Name Defense rose to the occasion. They knew their perfect record was on the line. Was it bye-bye to 17 and 0?

In desperation, Kilmer decided to try the long bomb. He went back to pass. But an awesome Dolphin blitz buried the 'Skins signal-caller. The ball never left his hand.

It was all over. Miami won Super Bowl VII 14-7. The 17-0 Dolphins had the best single-season record in the history of the NFL.

The Miami locker room was a madhouse after the victory. No one was happier than Coach Don Shula. He had already lost two Super Bowl games, one each as coach of the Baltimore Colts and the Dolphins.

"We won it for Shula," said Griese. "He lost two Super Bowls before. I'm happy for him."

Miami's No-Name Defense had stolen the show. Manny Fernandez seemed to be in on every Washington running play. Linebacker

Buoniconti was all over the field. And safety Jake Scott intercepted two Kilmer passes, returning them 63 yards. In a defensive battle like Super Bowl VII, it was no surprise that a defender like Scott was named MVP.

Miami	7	7	0	0	—	14
Wash	0	0	0	7	—	7

Miami—Twilley 28 pass from Griese
      (Yepremian kick)
Miami—Kiick 1 run (Yepremian kick)
Wash —Bass 49 fumble return (Knight kick)

SUPER BOWL
VI

MIAMI vs. DALLAS

One of the newest teams in the NFL made it to Super Bowl VI in New Orleans. The Miami Dolphins, the AFC champs, had been a team less than five years. To make it to the big game, the Dolphins earned a 27-24 play-off victory over the Kansas City Chiefs. It wasn't easy. The Dolphins didn't win until the sixth quarter! Talk about OT! Garo Yepremian's field goal ended the longest NFL game ever. The NFC representative was the Super Bowl loser from the year before, the Dallas Cowboys.

The game started out the wrong way for Miami. Bruising fullback Larry Csonka had carried over 200 times during the regular season without a single fumble. He picked a bad time for his first fumble. Dallas line-backer Chuck Howley recovered the ball at his own 46-yard line.

The Cowboys got started right away.

Dallas' Roger Staubach scrambles away from a Miami defender.

Running backs Duane Thomas and Walt Garrison pounded out yardage. QB Roger Staubach tossed short passes to Thomas and Garrison and tight end Mike Ditka. A field goal gave Dallas a quick 3-0 lead.

The Miami offense had trouble getting its own running game going. Their famous running backs, Larry Csonka and Jim Kiick, were getting nowhere against the Dallas "Doomsday" defense. On offense, Staubach picked the Miami defense apart. He hit veteran Lance Alworth for a TD to go up 10-0.

Late in the first half, Miami quarterback Bob Griese finally got his Dolphins rolling. Griese dropped back to pass. Wide receiver Paul Warfield, one of the greatest ever to play the game, was open across the middle. But this time the future Hall-of-Famer dropped it at the 2-yard line. The Dolphins settled for a 31-yard field goal. The first half ended Dallas 10, Miami 3.

The second half was more of the same. Speedy wideout Bob Hayes, the fastest man in the world, tough-as-nails tight end Mike Ditka, and the great Dallas rushing game were too much for the Miami defense. And the Doomsday Defense, led by Chuck Howley, held the Dolphins to the lowest point total in Super Bowl history! Dallas won going away, 24-3, to even their Super Bowl record at 1-1.

Roger Staubach completed 12 of 19 passes for 119 yards and two touchdowns. He also directed the Dallas running game to 252 big rushing yards. Duane Thomas led the runners with 95 yards. Walt Garrison had 74. For his leadership, Staubach was named the Most Valuable Player in Super Bowl VI.

| Dallas | 3 | 7 | 7 | 7 | — | 24 |
| Miami | 0 | 3 | 0 | 0 | — | 3 |

Dallas—FG Clark 9
Dallas—Alworth 7 pass from Staubach
    (Clark kick)
Miami—FG Yepremian 31
Dallas—Thomas 3 run (Clark kick)
Dallas—Ditka 7 pass from Staubach
    (Clark kick)

SUPER BOWL V

BALTIMORE vs. DALLAS

For the 1970 season, the 10 teams of the AFL merged with the 16 teams of the NFL. Two conferences were formed: the American Football Conference and the National Football Conference. Three old NFL teams transferred to the AFC: the Pittsburgh Steelers, Cleveland Browns and Baltimore Colts. That way, the AFC and the NFC each had 13 teams. Super Bowl V in Miami was the first to match the winners of the AFC and the NFC.

But the first winner of the AFC title was an old NFL team—the Colts! They would meet a team that would be making the first of many appearances in the Super Bowl—the high-powered Dallas Cowboys. This was Baltimore's second Super Bowl, after losing to Namath's Jets in Super Bowl III.

Before the kickoff, there was no hint that Super Bowl V would go down in history as the Blooper Bowl.

The Colts committed the first blooper early in the game. Quarterback Johnny Unitas completed a pass—to Dallas linebacker Chuck Howley. But the Cowboys couldn't capitalize on the break. The Colts were also guilty of the second blooper. Safety Ron Gardin went deep to receive a Dallas punt. He caught the ball, put on a fancy move and ran upfield. The only problem was he left the ball back on the 9-yard line! Dallas recovered and got a field goal for a 3-0 edge.

Then Cowboy QB Craig Morton took his team down to the Colt 6-yard line. But a penalty put the ball back to the 23-yard line. Instead of a touchdown, Dallas had to settle for another field goal. They led 6-0.

Baltimore cracked the scoreboard minutes later on one of the strangest plays in Super Bowl history. Unitas fired a deep pass to wide receiver Eddie Hinton. The ball bounced off Hinton's hands. Then it seemed to brush the fingertips of Dallas cornerback Mel Renfro. And then the ball fell into the arms of Baltimore tight end John Mackey. Mackey caught the deflected pass at midfield and ran in untouched for a touchdown.

If Renfro hadn't touched the ball, the play would have been illegal. That's because two offensive players couldn't touch a pass unless a defender touched it in between. But the

Baltimore ties the game at 13-13 in the fourth quarter.

UPI Photo

referees ruled the play good. And Baltimore had tied the score, 6-6. The score stayed tied, too. The Cowboys blocked the extra point kick by rookie Jim O'Brien.

The next Baltimore blooper, a Unitas fumble at the Baltimore 28-yard line, led to a Dallas TD. Dallas 13, Baltimore 6. But the Colts weren't through. Unitas was smashed by Dallas defensive end George Andrie as he threw a pass. The ball fluttered downfield and Dallas' Mel Renfro picked it off. But that wasn't the only bad news on the play. Unitas suffered a fractured rib on the hit by Andrie. He was finished for the day.

Backup quarterback Earl Morrall moved the Colts down to the Dallas 2-yard line with just seconds left in the half. Three running plays went nowhere. On fourth down, Morrall tried to hit tight end Tom Mitchell. But the Colts' bad luck continued. The pass was incomplete. Dallas kept its 13-6 lead at halftime.

The Baltimore bloopers continued in the third quarter. Jim Duncan took the second half kickoff for the Colts and fumbled the ball. The Cowboys recovered at the Baltimore 3-yard line. Morton handed off to running back Duane Thomas. But now it was Dallas' turn to say hello to Mr. Blooper! Thomas fumbled the ball back to the Colts at the 1-foot line.

Had he scored, it would have been 20-6 for Dallas. But the blooper kept the Colts in the game.

After the Colts made their final blooper, when linebacker Chuck Howley intercepted another Baltimore pass, Dallas took the bloopers. Halfway through the final period, Morton passed to Walt Garrison. The ball bounced off his fingertips. Baltimore safety Rick Volk intercepted and returned the ball to the Dallas 3-yard line. A touchdown and O'Brien's extra point tied the game 13-13.

Time was running out. If the game ended in a tie, the teams would go into sudden death. They would play until either team scored points on a touchdown, field goal, or safety. Which team would make the final blooper of Blooper Bowl V?

With less than two minutes left, the Cowboys were driving for the winning score. Morton set up to pass. He fired the ball. Interception! Baltimore linebacker Mike Curtis returned it to the Dallas 28-yard line. A couple of running plays knocked the clock down to less than 10 seconds.

The Baltimore field goal unit took the field. Every football fan in the world remembered that Jim O'Brien's first kick of the day had been blocked. The Cowboys remembered it, too. They called time out to psych out the rookie. Finally, the teams lined up. Morrall took the snap from center Bill Curry. He spotted the ball on the ground. O'Brien kicked the ball. The crowd went crazy.

The ball sailed between the goal posts! The Colts had won Super Bowl V 16-13. The rookie had come through. O'Brien's kick was one of the few plays that worked right in the Blooper Bowl. The Colts gave up three interceptions, lost four fumbles, and had a kick blocked. Dallas had three of its passes intercepted and lost that one critical fumble on the Baltimore 1-foot line. Dallas fans did have one victory to celebrate. Dallas linebacker Chuck Howley was named the MVP. He was the first and the only player from a losing team to win the MVP award.

Baltimore	0	6	0	10	—	16
Dallas	3	10	0	0	—	13

Dallas—FG Clark 14
Dallas—FG Clark 30
Balt —Mackey 75 pass from Unitas
         (kick blocked)
Dallas—Thomas 7 pass from Morton
         (Clark kick)
Balt —Nowatzke 2 run (O'Brien kick)
Balt —FG O'Brien 32

SUPER BOWL IV

KANSAS CITY vs. MINNESOTA

Super Bowl IV in New Orleans was to be the last Super Bowl for the AFL. The 10 AFL teams were going to join the National Football League for the 1970 season. After 10 years of play the AFL would disappear, becoming a conference, the AFC, in the bigger, older league.

The Kansas City Chiefs won the last AFL title. Super Bowl IV would be the second Super Bowl for the Chiefs. They had lost the very first Super Bowl game. Their opponents were the heavily favored Minnesota Vikings, called the Purple People-Eaters after the roughhouse defense they played. But KC's defense was also pretty tough.

As expected, defense controlled the early part of the game. Neither team was able to get much going. The Chiefs did put together one short drive in the opening period. QB Len Dawson moved his offense to the Minnesota

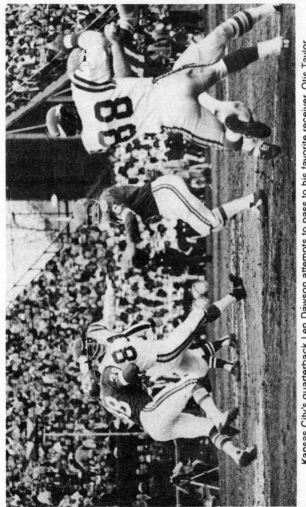

Kansas City's quarterback Len Dawson attempts to pass to his favorite receiver, Otis Taylor.

UPI Photo

41-yard line before the drive stalled. Jan Stenerud's Super Bowl-record 48-yard field goal gave the Chiefs a 3-0 lead. Two more KC drives stalled in Viking territory. But super booter Stenerud split the uprights twice more for a 9-0 lead.

To make matters worse for Minnesota, Viking Charlie West fumbled the kickoff. The Chiefs recovered at the Minnesota 19-yard line. But Dawson wasn't going to settle for yet another Stenerud FG. Running back Mike Garrett bowled over the goal line for the first touchdown of the game. The Chiefs took a 16-0 lead into the locker room. And the whole world was surprised at how easy it had looked so far.

Viking quarterback Joe Kapp finally got his offense rolling in the second half. A Dave Osborn touchdown closed the gap to 16-7. The Chiefs had another weapon that they had not used yet—all-pro receiver Otis Taylor. From the Minnesota 46-yard line, Dawson fired a short pass to Taylor. Minnesota cornerback Earsell Mackbee smacked Taylor. But it was Mackbee who fell. The fleet-footed Taylor went racing down the field. He turned a short pass into a breathtaking 46-yard touchdown! Kansas City had a 23-7 lead.

Minnesota's Mackbee had to be helped from the field following the collision with Otis

Taylor. "I pinched a nerve," he said after the game. "The arm went dead, and I couldn't grab him. That's how he got away."

The Vikings suffered an even bigger injury in the fourth period. Quarterback Joe Kapp rolled out to avoid the Kansas City rush. But defensive tackle Aaron Brown caught up with Kapp and smashed him to the ground. The Vikings quarterback left the field holding his injured left arm. He was finished for the day.

Gary Cuozzo took over as quarterback for the Vikings. But he had no better luck against the fired-up Chiefs. The Vikings never threatened again. Super Bowl IV ended with a 23-7 Kansas City victory. The win gave the Chiefs a 1-1 record in the Super Bowl and the AFL a 2-2 record in the big game. And Super Bowl IV started the Vikings on their way to a record four losses in the big game!

Len Dawson completed 12 of 17 passes for 142 yards and a touchdown. He was named MVP of Super Bowl IV. The Chiefs had two reasons to celebrate after the Super Bowl IV victory. They had earned revenge for the Super Bowl I defeat. And they had won the last Super Bowl for an AFL team.

K. C.	3	13	7	0	—	23
Minnesota	0	0	7	0	—	7

```
KC   —FG Stenerud 48
KC   —FG Stenerud 32
KC   —FG Stenerud 25
KC   —Garrett 5 run (Stenerud kick)
Minn—Osborn 4 run (Cox kick)
KC   —Taylor 46 pass from Dawson
        (Stenerud kick)
```

SUPER BOWL III

NEW YORK JETS vs. BALTIMORE

New York Jets quarterback Joe Namath did a lot of talking in the days before Super Bowl III in Miami. "Earl Morrall would be third-string quarterback on the Jets," said Namath of Baltimore's QB. "There are maybe five or six better quarterbacks than Morrall in the AFL."

That made some of the Colts angry.

"We're a better team than Baltimore," said Broadway Joe.

That made some of the Colts even angrier.

"I think we'll win it," said Namath. "In fact, I'll guarantee it."

That made some of the Colts angrier still. But it also made a lot of people laugh. The NFL's mighty Baltimore Colts were 18-point favorites over the New York Jets.

The Jets had rallied from behind to beat the Oakland Raiders 27-23 in the AFL championship game. But the Colts had rambled to a fine 13-1 regular season mark and a 34-zip whitewashing of the Cleveland Browns in the NFL title game. The Colts' defense was awesome, tops in the NFL. Earl Morrall had had a great year. They had every reason to be confident of victory!

Little did they know they would be part of one of the most famous football games ever played.

The game started slowly, each team trying to size up the other. The Colts knocked on the door several times in the first half. But interceptions and a missed field goal kept them from scoring.

Namath took advantage of an endzone interception. He started his offense from the New York 20-yard line. Namath sent bruising fullback Matt Snell time and again over offensive tackle Winston Hill. Hill cleared Colts Ordell Braase and Fred Miller from Snell's path. Snell knocked off five or six yards a crack.

Namath mixed in passes with Snell's runs. Broadway Joe passed twice to wide receiver George Sauer for 14 and 11 yards. On the 12th play of the drive, Namath again handed off to Snell, who burst over from four yards out. Touchdown! The football world was shocked as the Jets took a 7-0 lead into halftime.

The Colts had a great chance to even the

score with just 25 seconds left in the half. Morrall handed off to running back Tom Matte. Matte pitched the ball back to Earl Morrall. Wide receiver Jimmy Orr was all alone in the end zone. Orr jumped up and down, waving his arms. But Morrall never saw him. Instead he fired down the middle. The pass was picked off by Jet Jim Hudson.

"I was the primary receiver," said Orr after the game. "Earl said he just didn't see me. I was open from here (Miami) to Tampa."

The Colts continued to have problems early in the second half. On the first play of the third quarter, Matte fumbled. The New York Jets recovered. Several plays later, Jim Turner kicked a 32-yard field goal. New York increased its lead to 10-0 and the world held its breath. Were they about to watch one of the greatest upsets in history?

Snell continued to slice through the proud Baltimore defense. And Namath was able to pop short passes to George Sauer, Bill Mathis and tight end Pete Lammons. The Jet drive stalled at the Baltimore 23-yard line. Jim Turner came on and kicked a 30-yard field goal. 13-0, Jets!

Baltimore Coach Don Shula sent in a new quarterback on the next Colt possession. Veteran, but aging, superstar Johnny Unitas replaced Morrall late in the third period.

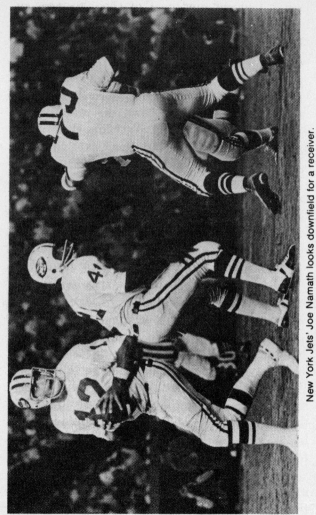

New York Jets' Joe Namath looks downfield for a receiver.

N.Y. Jets Photo

Unitas had sat out most of the 1968 season because of arm trouble. But he entered Super Bowl III in hopes of picking up the Baltimore offense.

The Jets got another field goal early in the fourth quarter for a shocking 16-0 lead. Midway through the final period, Unitas started hitting his receivers. "Johnny U" completed four straight passes in putting together the best Baltimore drive of the game. Fullback Jerry Hill scored from one yard out, cutting the New York lead to 16-7.

The Colts were successful on an onside kick. Unitas started another drive into New York territory. Fans knew that if anybody could stage a miracle comeback for the proud NFL, it was Unitas. But after completing three straight passes, he threw three incompletions. The Baltimore drive stalled. It was all over.

People had laughed when game MVP Joe Namath guaranteed the victory. They weren't laughing now. The Jets defeated the Colts by 16-7. The upstart American Football League had won its first Super Bowl game, beating the team that people thought couldn't be beaten. Namath completed 17 of 28 passes for 206 yards and no interceptions.

Some people called the New York victory a fluke. But Boadway Joe and his team came through—just as he promised. And the AFL had shown it could play football as well as that other league!

New York	0	7	6	3	—16
Baltimore	0	0	0	7	— 7

NY —Snell 4 run (Turner kick)
NY —FG Turner 32
NY —FG Turner 30
NY —FG Turner 9
Balt—Hill 1 run (Michaels kick)

SUPER BOWL II

OAKLAND vs. GREEN BAY

Coach Vince Lombardi's Pack was back to defend its Super Bowl title in Miami's Orange Bowl. The Oakland Raiders would represent the AFL. Some of the younger Raiders could remember swapping Bart Starr, Forrest Gregg, and Ray Nitschke football cards. "It's like playing against your father," said one of the Raiders. "These guys were my childhood heroes."

In the AFL title game, the Raiders had destroyed the Houston Oilers, 40-7. The NFL title game was played in weather 13 degrees below zero in frozen Wisconsin. The Dallas Cowboys held a 17-14 lead with time running out. On the last play of the game, Bart Starr kept the ball and dived over his offensive line for the winning touchdown. That Dallas-Green Bay game was called one of the greatest of all time. Some people wondered if the Packers could still get excited about another game.

They found out.

The Packers scored first. Quarterback Bart Starr drove his offense to a Don Chandler field goal. Green Bay had a 3-0 lead in the first quarter. Chandler kicked another field goal early in the second quarter, and Starr connected with Boyd Dowler for a 62-yard touchdown toss. Green Bay's lead was 13-0. Super Bowl II began to look like a massacre.

But the high-powered Oakland offense finally came to life. Quarterback Daryle Lamonica, nicknamed the Mad Bomber, fired a 23-yard TD pass to wide receiver Bill Miller, slashing the Green Bay lead to 13-7. The Oakland defense finally stopped the Packers, forcing Green Bay to punt. But Raider return man Rodger Bird fumbled the punt. Green Bay recovered near midfield and Chandler kicked a 43-yard field goal. Green Bay had a 16-7 edge at halftime.

The Packers added another touchdown and another field goal in the third quarter, pushing their lead to 26-7. But there was still worse to come for the Raiders. Packer cornerback Herb Adderly intercepted a Lamonica pass at his own 40-yard line. Picking up blocks from his defensive mates, Adderly went all the way for a 60-yard touchdown. 33-7, Green Bay!

Oakland added a TD in the fourth quarter, but it was too little, too late. Super Bowl II

ended in a Green Bay romp, 33-14. For the
second year in a row, Packer QB Bart Starr
was named MVP. But there was one more
surprise. Legendary Packer coach Vince
Lombardi announced that the game would be
his last as Packer head coach. He retired at
the top of the football world, knowing that he
had done it all.

Green Bay 3 13 10 7 — 33
Oakland   0   7   0 7 — 14

GB —FG Chandler 39
GB —FG Chandler 20
GB —Dowler 62 pass from Starr
        (Chandler kick)
Oak—Miller 23 pass from Lamonica
        (Blanda kick)
GB —FG Chandler 24
GB —Anderson 2 run (Chandler kick)
GB —Adderly 60 interception return
        (Chandler kick)
Oak—Miller 23 pass from Lamonica
        (Blanda kick)

KANSAS CITY vs. GREEN BAY

The date was January 15, 1967, the first Super Sunday ever. The place was the Los Angeles Coliseum. Never before had teams from the National Football League and American Football League been on the same field at the same time. The Green Bay Packers and Kansas City Chiefs were going to do battle in Super Bowl I. They played not only for themselves but for the honor of their leagues.

The NFL was the old, established league. The AFL was only seven years old. The NFL had tried for years to ignore the young AFL. But the new league started signing good college players. And the AFL started stealing veteran players from the old league. The NFL was forced to pay attention to the younger league. The NFL and AFL agreed to send their championship teams to meet in a season-ending football game. People started calling it the "Super Bowl." The name stuck.

Under Coach Vince Lombardi, the Packers had won four NFL titles in the past eight years. In 1966, the Pack swept to a 12-2 regular season record. Green Bay won the NFL title by edging the Dallas Cowboys, 34-27, in a classic game. The Chiefs earned the right to represent the AFL by defeating the Buffalo Bills.

Winning alone wasn't going to be enough for some of the Packers. "We have to show clearly just how big a difference there is between the two teams," said defender Lionel Aldridge. "One touchdown won't be enough."

The Packers and Chiefs took the field on a warm, sunny day. They were about to make pro football history.

Green Bay quarterback Bart Starr got his offense going halfway through the first quarter. From the Kansas City 37-yard line, Starr set up to pass. Starr threw deep to receiver Max McGee. TD! Green Bay led 7-0. Kansas City's offense made its move early in the second period. Quarterback Len Dawson found that short passes would work against the Green Bay defense. He hit Mike Garrett and Otis Taylor during a long drive. Then fullback Curtis McClinton hauled in a pass and rumbled in for a touchdown. The Chiefs surprised the football world by tying the score at 7-7.

Green Bays' Bart Starr barks the signals in the very first Super Bowl game.

The Packers struck right back. Starr drove the Pack 73 yards in 13 plays for the go-ahead score. Fullback Jim Taylor scored the touchdown on a famous Packer power sweep. Green Bay led 14-7. But late in the half, Dawson used his short passing offense to drive the Chiefs to a field goal. The Pack held a narrow 14-10 lead as the first half ended.

"We were a little too cautious in the first half," said Packer defensive end Willie Davis. "I figured, forget Kansas City and the Super Bowl and do what you do best."

The third quarter was all Green Bay. The Pack came out smoking! By the time the dust cleared, they had scored twice to take a commanding 28-10 lead. Another TD in the fourth quarter, and that's all she wrote! The Packers had won the first Super Bowl 35-10 and defended the honor of the NFL against the upstart AFL. Bart Starr was named the first Most Valuable Player in Super Bowl history. He hit on 16 of 23 passes for 250 yards and two touchdowns.

The Chiefs were defeated but not silenced. "They made mistakes," said running back Mike Garrett. "They are not superhumans. We just made more mistakes."

But on that first Super Sunday, the Chiefs found out how far they—and the AFL—had to go to match up with the now legendary

Green Bay Packers!

| K. C | | 0 | 10 | 0 | 0 | — 10 |
| Green Bay | 7 | 7 | 14 | 7 | — 35 |

GB—McGee 37 pass from Starr
    (Chandler kick)
KC—McClinton 7 pass from Dawson
    (Mercer kick)
GB—Taylor 14 run (Chandler kick)
KC—FG Mercer 31
GB—Pitts 5 run (Chandler kick)
GB—McGee 13 pass from Starr
    (Chandler kick)
GB—Pitts 1 run (Chandler kick)

SUPER BOWL RECORDS

SCORING

Most Points, Game
18, Roger Craig, San Francisco, XIX; Jerry Rice, San Francisco, XXIV

Most Touchdowns, Game
3, Roger Craig, San Francisco, XIX; Jerry Rice, San Francisco, XXIV

Most Field Goals, Game
4, Don Chandler, Green Bay, II; Ray Wersching, San Francisco, XVI

Longest Field Goal
48 yards, Rich Karlis, Denver, XXI,
Jan Stenerud, Kansas City, IV

RUSHING

Most Yards Gained, Game
204, Timmy Smith, Washington, XXII

Longest Gain
74, Marcus Allen, Los Angeles Raiders, XVIII

PASSING

Most Yards Gained, Game
357, Joe Montana, San Francisco, XXIII

Longest Completion
80, Jim Plunkett (to Kenny King), Oakland, XV
80, Doug Williams (to Ricky Sanders),
Washington, XXII

Most Touchdown Passes, Game
5, Joe Montana, San Francisco, XXIV

RECEIVING

Most Receptions, Game
11, Dan Ross, Cincinnati, XVI; Jerry Rice, San Francisco, XXIII

Most Yards Gained, Game
215, Jerry Rice, San Francisco, XXIII

INTERCEPTIONS

Most Interceptions, Game
3, Rod Martin, Oakland, XV
Longest Return
60 yards, Herb Adderley, Green Bay, II

PUNTING

Longest Punt
62, Rich Camarillo, New England, XX
Highest Punting Average, Game
48.5 yards, Jerrel Wilson, Kansas City, IV

RETURNS

Longest Punt Return
45, John Taylor, San Francisco, XXIII
Longest Kickoff Return
98, Fulton Walker, Miami, XVII

TEAM SCORING

Most Points, Game
55, San Francisco, XXIV
Fewest Points, Game
3, Miami, VI

TOTAL OFFENSE

Most Yards Gained, Game
602, Washington, XXII
Fewest Yards Gained, Game
119, Minnesota, IX

TOTAL DEFENSE

Fewest Yards Allowed, Game
119, Pittsburgh, IX
Fewest Points Allowed, Game
3, Dallas, VI

ANSWERS TO SUPER BOWL QUIZ

1. Pittsburgh Steelers: 4 times, IX, X, XIII, XIV.
   San Francisco 49ers: 4 times, XVI, XIX,
   XXIII, XXIV.

2. Dallas Cowboys: 5 times, V, VI, X, XII, XIII.
   Miami Dolphins: 5 times, VI, VII, VIII, XVII,
   XIX.
   San Francisco 49ers: XIII, XXIV.

3. Green Bay Packers: I, II;
   Miami Dolphins: VII, VIII;
   Pittsburgh Steelers: IX, X, XIII, XIV.

4. Most: XIII, Total of 66 points scored.
   Fewest: VII, 21 points.

5. Bart Starr, Green Bay Packers I, II;
   Terry Bradshaw, Pittsburgh Steelers, XIII,
   XIV.
   Joe Montana, San Francisco 49ers, XVI,
   XIX, XXIV.

6. Chuck Howley, Dallas Cowboys, V.

7. Super Bowl XII, Harvey Martin and Randy
   White, Dallas Cowboys.

8. Joe Montana, San Francisco 49ers, XXIV,
   5 TD passes.

9. The Orange Bowl in Miami, 5 times.

10. Minnesota Vikings, Pittsburgh Steelers,
    Denver Broncos, Dallas Cowboys,
    Miami Dolphins.